ALAN PATON

—COLLECTED POEMS—

Songs of Africa

GECKO BOOKS

Songs of Africa: collected poems of Alan Paton
© Gecko Books 1995

ISBN: Collector's Edition: 1-875011-20-X
Standard Edition: 1-875011-15-3

First published 1995 by
Gecko Books cc
21 Hereward Road
Durban 4001

Cover by Lesley Lewis of Inkspots
Design and desktop publication by Lesley Lewis of Inkspots.
Printed by Kohler Carton and Print, Pinetown.

ACKNOWLEDGEMENTS

THIS collection of poems could not have been compiled without the help of Joicelyn Leslie-Smith, the Manuscript Librarian at the Alan Paton Centre in Pietermaritzburg. Her patience with my endless queries, her extensive knowledge of the manuscript material and her enthusiasm for the whole project were an inspiration, and I am enormously grateful to her. Edward Callan, Distinguished University Professor Emeritus of Western Michigan University in Kalamazoo, is probably the most eminent authority on Alan's work. He has been unstinting in his advice and assistance, especially with the organisation of the poems, and his introduction is a most valuable contribution. I cannot thank him enough for his wise counsel and encouragement. I am most grateful to Douglas Livingstone, poet and friend, who, in his foreword, writes of Alan with such sincerity, deep understanding and knowledge; to Professor Colin Gardner for his help in deciphering some doubtful pieces of Alan's handwriting; to my agent and friend Frances Bond, a specialist in ironing out problems and coping with temperament; to Veronica Klipp and Gertrud Strauss of Gecko Books, whose expertise and enthusiasm have made the production of this book a pleasurable experience; and finally to the editor, Peter Kohler, who has pulled it all together. It is Peter who has given shape and form to my original concept of the book, and his painstaking and scholarly research unearthed previously unknown material.

And of course, without Alan there would not have been a book at all.

Anne Paton
August 1995

The publisher is grateful to David Philip for permission to reproduce poems from *Knocking on the Door* (1975).

Cover: Thanks to Joe Alfers for permission to use his photograph of Alan Paton on his 80th birthday.

Page xxxi (Alan Paton with dog): detail from photograph of staff and senior students 1921 (University of Natal Archives)

The publisher is grateful to the Alan Paton Centre, University of Natal, for permission to reproduce the following poems from the original manuscripts:

'To Walt Whitman' (Anerley 8 August 1948, p.66); 'I Take This Africa' (1950, p.70); 'The Joke' (Diary 1949, p.80); 'I ask you, Indian people...' (p.80); 'Black Woman Teacher' (14 September 1949, p.84), 'I am the Law' (25-26 February 1970, p.88); 'Necklace of Fire' (1986 version, p.94).

Thanks to Natal Newspapers for permission to use the photograph from the rehearsal for *Mkhumbane* (May 1960, p.100).

CONTENTS

FOREWORD BY DOUGLAS LIVINGSTONE   ix

INTRODUCTION BY EDWARD CALLAN   xxi

ALAN PATON — A CHRONOLOGY   xxxii

SONGS OF AFRICA

FIRST JOURNEY — BEGINNINGS

EARLY IMPRESSIONS

To a Picture   2
The Sea   3
Sonnet — To Sleep   5
Song of the Northward-Bound   6

COLLEGE POEMS

Old walls . . .   9
School   10
Trilemma   11
Memories 1919-1924   12

POEMS OF SETTLEMENT AND HISTORY

Ladysmith   14
The grass-larks' call . . .   15
Maritzburg in February   16
The farmers know . . .   17

SECOND JOURNEY — AWAKENING

POEMS OF DESIRE AND REDEMPTION

You and I —   20
Sonnet   22
To —   23
Gemellia   24
Sister Street   25

The Prostitute 26
Scottsville, 1931 27
Poor Whites 28
The Prodigals 29
Maria Lee 30
Sanna 32
The Prison House 33
Sonnet — To Sleep 34
The blood poured . . . 35
This love is warm . . . 35
To a Small Boy Who Died at Diepkloof Reformatory 36

TRANSLATIONS AND TRANSITIONS
Sonnet 38
Old Til 39
Felip 41
The Poet 44
The Future 45
The Bull-frog 46
Translation 47
Lied van die Verworpenes 48

SONGS OF DISCOVERY AND AFFIRMATION
Reverie 49
House of Dreams 50
Song 51
Tugela, Tugela, sweep on . . . 52
Carton 53
Sonnet 54
From where the sun pours . . . 54
Singer of Childhood 55
In the Umtwalumi Valley 56
The mist comes down . . . 57
I came to a valley . . . 58
I Have Approached 65
To Walt Whitman 67

THIRD JOURNEY — POEMS OF CONSCIENCE

POLITICS AND PHILANTHROPY
I Take This Africa 70
We Mean Nothing Evil Towards You 71
Could You Not Write Otherwise? 73
The Laughing Girls 74
The Discardment 75

iv

Dancing Boy 76
Indian Woman 77
The Stock Exchange 77
Durban 78
To a Person Who Fled to Rhodesia 79
I ask you, Indian people . . . 81
Anxiety Song of an Englishman 81
To a Black Man Who Lost a Child Thro' Starvation 82
Black Woman Teacher 85
Samuel 86
The Monument 87
I'll stab the conscience . . . 87
I am the Law . . . 89
Death of a Priest 91
Caprivi Lament 92
Necklace of Fire 95

PRAISES AND ELEGIES
On the Death of J.H. Hofmeyr 96
To Edgar Brookes 97
Praise Song for Luthuli 98
Flowers for the Departed 99

SONGS FROM THE MUSICAL MKHUMBANE
Opening Chorus 100
Morning Song 101
How the Enemy Ran! 103
Children's Song 104
He's Looking for Work 106
Factory Medley 107
Tsotsi Song 108
Who Will You Marry? 109
But Now They Don't Laugh Any More 110
Young Love 112
Song 113
Bantustan 114
Be Satisfied 116
Closing Song 116

FOURTH JOURNEY — SPIRITUAL EXERCISES

MEDITATIONS
Faith 118
Meditation for a Young Boy Confirmed 120

PSALMS AND DEVOTIONAL VERSE

No Place for Adoration	127
My Lord has a great attraction . . .	128
What is this sound . . .	129
A Psalm of the Forest	130
Heavy with secret knowledge . . .	131
For the earth is corrupted . . .	133
Oh Lord, my enemies overwhelm me . . .	134

PRAYERS

O Lord give me that grace . . .	135
Prayer	136
A Daily Prayer for One's Work	137

FIFTH JOURNEY — INDULGENCES

HUMOUR AND SATIRE

"No responsibility accepted.". . . . .Ed.	140
The Hermit	141
My Sense of Humour	142
The Chief	143
The Joke	144
Once in the Tavern . . .	144
My Great Discovery	145
Dr Verwoerd my boss . . .	149

INFORMAL WRITINGS

OCCASIONAL VERSE

Hail to the Chief	150
Prologue	151
For Ray Swart's Fiftieth Birthday	152
New Year's Eve 1982 at the Swarts'	153

LIGHT VERSE

There was a sweet family, Thorrold . . .	155
Annual Report of the S.P.C.G., Year Ending October, 1923.	156
Curlilocks . . .	157
There's memory of laughter . . .	157
Night is dark . . .	157
It's quite clear . . .	158
A knock there comes . . .	158
The New Physics	158
We Cogitate	162
Bus Passenger	162
The K.L.M.	163

Confused . . . 163
To Marion. 18.12.60 164
It has been said . . . 164
Ode to the New Reality 165

POEMS FOR CHILDREN
Who Likes Me? 166
I can see Kitty 166
Hal 167

LAST JOURNEY — RETURN

REFLECTIONS
Sonnet 170
Sterility 171
Evening 171
When the last sleep comes . . . 172
Retreat! Retreat! . . . 173
The Incurable 174
Death 175
Only the Child Is No More 176
The world is changing too fast for me . . . 177
1950-1984 177

ALTERNATIVE VERSIONS AND OTHER WORKINGS
I saw in a dream . . . 178
I'll sting the conscience . . . 179
The Incurable 180
The tributary widens . . . 182
Necklace of Fire 182

NOTES 185

NOTES ON CONTRIBUTORS 202

EDITOR'S AFTERWORD 203

INDEX OF FIRST LINES 215

FOREWORD

Alan Paton and the Logos: a few notes and personal recollections

by Douglas Livingstone

LOGOS: even the word presented us with some initial problems. To Alan Paton its prime import and impact were profoundly Christian, stemming presumably from those 3 or 4 passages of the Johannine canon in the New Testament; to me, while conceding possibly metaphysical dimensions, the word was a lower case word pertaining primarily to words of reason. In time, as we got to know each other and became less serious with each other, the word appeared to settle somewhere in the middle ground of "literary discourse". But it remained a serious word for him as long as I knew him: it always retained at least a hint of the upper case.

MY first encounter with Alan was inauspicious, but not without its comical aspects. It was during the late 60s or early 70s, and the occasion was one of the remarkable Professor Elizabeth Sneddon's "Communication in Action" cultural jamborees at the University of Natal. I found myself — on my back foot, as it were — sharing a platform with a clutch of distinguished heavyweights among whom were Athol Fugard, Jon Stallworthy, André Brink and others (not Alan). The subject was "The Function of the Creative Artist in a Technological Society". (That word *Function*, I felt, was an even more insidious torpedo with a proximity fuse than *Technological*.) I suspected that I was there as the materialistic fall-guy, representing the Philistines, the crass scientist-technologist trampling the host of golden daffodils under his Brave New World-shod boots.

Sure enough, variations on the same old CP Snow job began to manifest themselves: only the Creative Artist had a soul; only the Creative Artist was blessed with a sort of transcendental miner's lamp for guiding benighted humanity out of the materialistic gloom into those illuminated and spiritual realms to which Creative Artists were naturally privy. There were not a few jocular asides about stolid hulks perched on lab stools staring fixedly at dials and meters or racks of test tubes, squinting into microscopes, or locked in a St Vitus' dance (choreographed by C Chaplin) tending conveyor belts and voracious machines.

It was an open invitation. In my turn, I implored the audience to support and nurture their scientists and technologists who made sure society's mundane wheels did not come off, and that typhoid did not issue from the water taps, and that when they — the audience — all went home and flipped the light switch, the lights would come on; that they could safely ignore the Creative Artist as the ultimate lightweight contributing little to ordinary living, human survival and the public weal.

As the uproar subsided, a scarlet visage surfaced in the audience: "Where do you get that horrible word 'lightweight' from, and how can you possibly apply it to a serious artist?"

"It's a category in boxing and wrestling," was my facetious reply.

Visibly enraged, I think as much by the fickle laughter of the audience, he was about to say more, but somebody next to him appeared to pull him back to his seat. "Who's the curmudgeon?" I asked someone. And was told.

✳✳✳

AFTERWARDS, over drinks in Professor Sneddon's library, we learned he should have been on the platform with us but had been away when the invitations went out. As it became clear that he had indeed been invited as a panellist, the intelligence mollified him. It was on this occasion, too, that I first met his wife Anne, and was immediately conscious of a woman of strength and capability, completely devoted to her husband's wellbeing. She smoothed his remaining ruffled feathers with brisk skill. I was swiftly (far quicker than Alan ever did) and silently assessed as not presenting any serious threat, of not being an enemy to the beloved country's leading literary luminary, and she left us to it. I soon learned: if she was convinced he would come to no harm, Anne had no problem in letting him off the leash.

✳✳✳

I BECAME at once aware of certain rigidities in him. He had a Calvinistic air and the unbending mien of the interrogative headmaster; there was, too, the brook-no-frivolity gravitas of the middle-echelon civil servant. But I was fortunate: I had the opportunity to learn there was more to him than this forbidding carapace.

I must have created an even worse impression: apparently my performance on the platform was a betrayal, if not of the Logos then of some sort of Sacred Calling. Much as I admired the great prose talent admonishing me in a corner of a Durban library that evening, keepers of public morals and earthbound recording angels have always brought out the worst in me. I went into my usual song and dance act of bad puns and inventive vulgarity.

When I focussed on his face again, I saw he was grinning at me crookedly, that grin of his that was almost a grimace. It could be that the heads side on the coin of Calvinism is balanced by more than a whiff of earthiness. Perhaps it was from this more or less suppressed side to his character that his inordinate love of poetry arose. Alan loved poetry — I was to learn later — with a rare and untidy passion.

✳✳✳

TO my amazement (and probably to his), the seeds of a close friendship were planted at that initial encounter and, in time, I became very fond of the man, as indeed I tend to do with most creative souls, believing them to be more cursed than blessed in their confrontation and attempted ordering of experience within a malevolent if magnificent creation. The unexamined life may not be worth living, but those who gaze not upon their navels have always struck me as being the happier. For want of a better word, the "circumference" of our friendship was limited due to circumstances and my own clumsiness. Limiting circumstances were: he had or appeared to have *time*, a commodity to which I, as an overstretched environmental scientist, had little access during the day; and most of our association was by telephone, a medium that tends to invite glibness, the flip response, not much reflection. Perhaps, too, at that time in the beloved country, there was a vague aura of bravado, a not quite conscious hope that one was bamboozling/ impressing/ entertaining/ educating/ insulting any ears of state that might be plugged into the phone network. (Of course, the immense boon of the telephone — its immediacy — is offset by its usurpation of immortal and later-to-be-dissected literary friendships conducted by letter.)

✳✳✳

SOMETIMES, Alan would phone me at the laboratory once or twice a week for months on end, the subject invariably a word, a poem, a literary reference — the logos with a small "l".

"Mnah. You busy?"
"Hello, Alan. Yes."

"Been in the sea?"

"Yes."

"Some call it work! What do you make of the word *scintilla*?"

"I cannot believe you haven't a dictionary, or indeed several."

"OK. But what does it mean to you?"

"You mean as in 'Scintillate, scintillate, globule vivific ...'?"

"As in 'Twinkle, twinkle, little star ...'?"

"That's the one. Maybe scintilla is a hint of a twink."

"You never fail to disappoint me."

$$* * *$$

AT King's School, Nottingham Road, the genial headmaster of that (at the time) bravely multiracial endeavour, John Mitchell, poured scotch, bustling hospitably about his office ministering to a select gathering: Alan, several of his ex-Liberal Party cronies and one interloper.

When the Sons of the Pioneers assemble, the Tamed Colonial Boys foregather, certain rituals seem to prevail. First, feet apart, facing into the circle, drink in right hand, left hand (if you are not a smoker) behind the back or pocketed; the conversation tends to be muted and innocuous, the degree of shared acquaintance ranging from old friends to the newly introduced. After about the third drink, the voices are louder, the feet further apart; acquaintanceship, however recent, is now presumed upon, and, here and there, the wedding guest is fixed if not transfixed by a calculating and glittering eye that has zeroed in — radar like — on its uncomfortable quarry: the room now seems crowded with ancient mariners, each of whose previously immobilised left hand has been replaced by a barely controllable iron clamp or steel hook. At a still later stage, the feet tend to assume the classic boxer's stance: left, slightly forward; right, a little behind; there is a vaguely pugilistic, if muted, rhythmic lunging motion of the torso; gruff and manly insults are cheerfully exchanged. I have seen this phenomenon all over Africa, among all nationalities, wherever men are gathered together, away from the women. The paradigm may obtain in the northern hemisphere as well.

On that evening, most of us were well into the final stages, and Alan and I were verbally slugging it out to what appeared to be the huge delight of the assembly. A late-comer happened to arrive during a particularly outrageous exchange and, appalled at my lese-majesty, seized my left bicep and said, "Do you know who you are talking to? *That's* Alan Paton!" Alan reacted swiftly and with anger: "Do you know who *you* are talking to? Do not interfere here." The well-meaning unfortunate slunk off. The strict rules for admittance to the Company of Men had been preserved: the initiations cannot be circumvented or bypassed.

✳✳✳

IN the parochial little world at the southern end of the heart-shaped continent, isolated and quarantined by the rest of humanity, Alan represented one of Whitey's few passports to respectability in several global forums: he was a solitary cultural lighthouse in the South African twilight, the natural corollary being his presence was much sought after to grace the village pump. There could be no doubt that he was an international literary lion, but that did not let him off the local circuit; if "they" (the locals) could have, "they" would have had him opening church bazaars. Here, Anne came into her own shielding him from the importunate. And here, I was elected as a stalking horse: one of the few whom Anne — standing at the telephone with the metaphorical sword of St Michael aloft — allowed direct access to her husband.

Invitations to address schools, cultural bodies and tertiary students were passed on by me, although I did exercise a bit of filtering myself. He felt obliged to accept as many as possible, despite a growing despair over the shrinking choice of new subjects. To a lesser degree, I was being sucked into or onto a similar treadmill. One day, approached by a school, he could not make it; so I was hauled in as a substitute. There being barely time enough, I stipulated: no lectures; I would read a few poems; and I would take questions at the end. To my surprise and probably everyone else's, this worked. Discussing it later with Alan, he fell upon the ploy with alacrity and joy; thereafter, he would happily present himself at lecture theatres and halls with a clutch of his favourite poems and entertain his audience and himself reading them with a sort of shy gusto.

✳✳✳

MEETINGS in the flesh were not that frequent: perhaps 4 or 5 dinner parties over the years out at the Paton's place at Botha's Hill where there were always other guests so everyone behaved with proper suburban civility, although there were the inevitable political discussions in which I participated little because I tend to take a bleakly biological view of "politics". Elsewhere, we bumped into each other three or four times a year at local lectures and talks, occasionally sharing the same public platform. During breaks and intervals, he had a trick of manoeuvring himself so that I obscured Anne's line of sight to him and he would

xiv

sneak a couple of surreptitious drags from my (in those days, inevitable) cigarette.

***

THERE were some words over which we had some amusingly fierce discussions. One was "liberal". I think he had early and elliptically decided I was politically naive, such unsophistication possibly to be attended to later. When "liberal" arose, I told him I regarded him as a Liberal with a capital L; he could regard me, I told him lightly, as a liberal with a small l. He accepted this with equanimity for a while. Then he phoned me to challenge me for definitions, differences. A Political Discussion loomed — a pastime I have ever regarded as palpitatingly exciting and as relevant to suffering humanity as postal chess, and told him so. His anger was swift, and he suggested that I should rather be labelled a Libertine "with a capital L" (— we already knew something of each other's past scrapes). When I laughed, he put the phone down. After one of our "differences", he would invariably phone in a day or two his indirect forgiveness — indirect in that the subject of the call would be a new one, a fresh arena. I would mischievously raise the old subject, the contretemps. He would grandly cut me short signifying my aberration had been noted; the caravan had to move on; he bore me no grudge over my character deficiencies and ratiocinative shortcomings.

***

IT is common knowledge that Alan had an enormous appetite for politics. I could not share in this. As a boy of 9 or 10, I had experienced the adult world of realpolitik in the shape of the Imperial Nipponese Army in Malaya. Growing up in Africa, attracted to the perhaps old-fashioned field of the naturalist, studying microbiology, working in the laboratories of bush hospitals, there gradually grew in me an implacable loathing for death, disease, contamination of the planet, suffering inflicted on any lifeform. Voluntary politicians were dangerous children without talent, with time on their hands, hardly more than 2-dimensional cutout paper clowns tap dancing on skulls in a crimson-lit box, an insane child's toy theatre. What is real enough is the mountains of human misery they and their craven apparatchiks manage to excrete.

When the inevitable "let's have our cards on the table" probe eventually arose in our association — what were my politics — my response was clumsy to a degree, limiting our dialogue ever afterwards. There were no authentic politics, I said, except the politics of the bacteriological culture plate; dog eat dog; survival of the most powerful, the most vicious. We should be governed solely by people of immense talent who loathed politics, who should be coerced, dragged kicking and screaming into the role of governance. Anyone who *wanted* to be a politician should by definition be excluded as an aberrant soul. Alan listened to me in silence and never raised the subject directly again. Discussion of political scandals and related generalizations arose inevitably enough, but these were more or less relegated by a bon mot or two, or the dismissive epithet: "Bloody government". As I say, the limitation, the clumsiness was mine.

✳✳✳

"MNAH. I've got to give another bloody talk."
"Eternal Verities?"
"Yes."
"You're so good at it. You must be the Eternal Verities guru around here."
"You are an unsympathetic bastard."
"Read 'em some 'pomes'."
"I was hoping you'd say that. What 'pomes'?"
"'Tiger! Tiger! ...'"
As long as I knew him, he maintained Blake's 'Tiger' was the greatest poem ever penned.

✳✳✳

THIS word "Mnah" perhaps needs some explanation. It is my phonetic rendering of the monosyllabic sound, invariably the first he uttered on the phone. I believe it stood for "(It's) M(e): A(lan)", with the n transposed to behind the M. After working this out, I put it to him with an explanatory theory: our ridiculous embarrassment at using our own names to announce ourselves. He found all this very funny, but did not stop using it. "Mnah." It's a noise I still miss, at the other end of the phone.

✳✳✳

THERE were other folk he consulted over words, others that I knew about: his friend the eminent critic Tony Morphet, his son Jonathan, a respected scholar and a talented writer in his own right, several academics on the Pietermaritzburg and Durban campuses and possibly further afield, and there were others — literary, political and religious friends.

xvi

Comparing notes then and later with several of them, I have the impression that I was reserved for jovial verbal recreation: he expended energy in trying to trip me up; also, that he would have been disappointed if he had succeeded in intimidating me into the almost universal genuflections he was received with at the time. The nearest I ever came to becoming conscious of a possible dislocation in our respective roles occurred a couple of times when my own inward gaze uneasily rested on the question: "Who is the real court jester here?"

"Mnah. What do you make of the word *selcouth*?"
"Sounds like a marriage between 'seldom' and 'uncouth'."
"Meaning?"
"I'm guessing now: like the Scots 'unco', sort of 'uncommon'."
"You never fail to disappoint me."

✳✳✳

HIS normally dry sense of humour could sharpen into the impish, and further, into the fairly lacerating. A couple of examples (at my expense) may serve to illustrate this. A review of one of my slim volumes caught his eye and he phoned asking where he could get a copy. Naturally, I sent a copy off to him immediately. A few days later he phoned with a "wait-for-it-this-is-going-to-kill-you" energy in his voice to say: "Thank you for your book of poems. I shall waste no time in reading it." Then he laughed, and repeated the joke to make sure I'd got it. I told him coldly I had got the joke, but I did not think it was original. After a pause, he agreed it probably wasn't.

Another time he phoned to tell me someone had referred to me as "'our silver-tongued poet'. And I said to them: 'Are you sure you don't mean our poet with the *silver-plated* tongue?'" Chuckles all round.

And once, during a symposium on Roy Campbell, sharing a platform with Archbishop Denis Hurley, Professor Colin Gardner and Alan, I mispronounced a word. As usual, I was obsessively swept up into associative games in my skull as the word "gyre" (correctly pronounced) was mentioned by one of the speakers, and I recalled how Roy had rhymed "gyre" with "fire" just as Yeats had some years earlier in 'Sailing to Byzantium', and how I had always used it with a hard g when quoting the first stanza of Lewis Carroll's 'Jabberwocky', and again with a hard g in Walter Scott's marvellously chilling "gyre-carline" — a queen witch or ogress. When I had to use the word myself a little later aloud that evening, "gyre" came out with a hard g. Alan at once and with enormous relish corrected me, much to the amusement of the audience. Doubtless this was a fitting levelling of the score from our first peppery encounter.

✳✳✳

ALAN'S trajectory of enthusiasm for the projected Campbell biography seemed to traverse the incandescence of liftoff to fizzle quite rapidly. We had several fairly intensive discussions about this. There is no doubt that there were difficulties of time, his own writing commitments, and so on. However, he relinquished the project not because his sensibilities were shocked by the affaire between Mary and Victoria, as some have suggested, but because of what he regarded as the devastating effect on Roy's subsequent work. Once, he asked me where I stood on the matter. I replied I always took the side of lovers whatever their sex or the sequence of events or cost of their passions and agonies. "Even at the expense of Art?" he demanded. When I said yes, it was implied for several weeks I had failed an important test.

✳✳✳

OVER the years we had frequent consultations on his Poetry Reading List for Public Occasions. 'Tiger' remained top of the pops. I think he read it every time he appeared on a public platform when poems were on the menu. He used to start the piece almost mechanically, then the wonder of the language or his own inner vision possessed him and he seemed to become entranced. Here, indeed, was a manifestation of the Logos: the respectful man, nonetheless firm, spiritedly questioning his Maker on the mystery of cruelty in creation. I had the impression that while Alan regarded the Assisi as fraternal, a fellow soul on a plateau of (just) achievable elevation, the Blake of 'The Tiger' represented a rarefied peak of human spirituality forever unattainable, an impossible summit forever to be striven after, a more powerful lure even than the Christ — Blake not having had the advantage of divine parentage in his interlocutions with his Creator.

Of course, I had to tease him: "Blake's not a poet ..." (this was received with growls) "... a visionary, a prophet, maybe a secular saint, but no poet. And there's some mighty creaky grammar in 'Tiger'." I think we both enjoyed Alan's ensuing outburst.

✳✳✳

HE once asked me if I agreed 'Tiger' was the best poem ever written. "Only if you've had a comfortable life," (overturning several tables). "Are you serious?" "Sure." "You talk the most utter rubbish. What if you've had an uncomfortable life?" "'Innisfree'," (there went several more tables). "You mean Yeats?" "Yes." "What rubbish." But he came back on the phone soon enough to crow: "Nine bean rows! You can't feed a family on nine bean rows." "Hang on there, William! I mean Alan. The man is alone in the poem; and there's honey as well. Besides, each bean row could be a mile long. Feed a bloody regiment." He expressed grave reservations about Irish metaphysicians and microbiologists' tastes in poetry but, in time, 'Innisfree' entered the repertoire.

On every occasion, I suggested he should include 'Diepkloof', which always pleased him although he tried to disguise this. "I shall read it, but I will tell them *you* said I must read it." "They will thank me."

✳✳✳

WAS Alan a great poet, or even a "good" one? His passion for poetry was certainly prodigious; at times — it must be allowed — his reach exceeded his grasp. It never ceased to amaze me that a deployer of such sublime prose, a consummate master, would so hunger after the more frivolous and vatic fifth dimension of verse as a channel for self expression. Perhaps dissatisfaction with achieved terrain is a signifier of the authentic creative spirit.

'Diepkloof' is, I believe, his best poem; although it includes many of the self evident rectitudes particular to the South African liberal inscape, it nonetheless works as a poem. Much of South African creative writing seems to be torn between lyricism and witness. Understandably so, perhaps. As a result of our history, witness tends to overshadow lyricism, overwhelming the landscape of dangerous beauty, the miraculous loves and friendships that thrust and twine and flower through ostensibly impossible barriers, the heedless continent that has to be gentled somehow into our human psyche. As an African species, we are — all of us — in desperate need of this transfiguring osmosis.

Yes, Alan Paton was a great poet — in his best prose. *Cry* is a magnificent prose poem that, in another age, dimension or solar system, could rival *Job* for a place in the canon of any Old Testament. And there is a most accomplished surgeon-poet weaving his ruthless magic behind elements of *Phalarope* and certain of the short stories. The present collection may serve as a source book, indicating some of the seeds and nurture of the great prose.

✳✳✳

"Mnah. I've just found a poem."
"By whom?"
"Walter de la Mare."
"Trouble with ole Wal is that splendid, usually gnomic opening stanza, usually dissolving into wilful or flummoxed obscurities ..."
"For God's sake, man, don't spoil it — and you're supposed to be a Celt! I'll phone again when you're not so busy."

✳✳✳

BACK from the beach and the early morning collection of marine samples, I pace from centrifuge to microscope; or stand with petri dish in one hand and culture loop in the other. The laboratory sings in silence. The phone no longer rings with an insistent voice from Botha's Hill at the other end.

I miss you, my friend.

©Douglas Livingstone 1995

INTRODUCTION

The Poems of Alan Paton: Longing for Home

by Edward Callan

> Simple I was, I wished to write but words,
> And melodies that had no meanings but their music
> And songs that had no meaning but their song.
> But the deep notes and the undertones
> Keep sounding themselves, keep insistently
> Intruding themselves, like a prisoned tide
> That under the shining and the sunlit sea
> In caverns and corridors goes underground
>   thundering.

('Could you not write otherwise?')

Inside Alan Paton, in whatever role we envision him — teacher, penal reformer, biographer, novelist, or foe of apartheid — there was always a lyric poet hoping to sing his way out. From childhood, Paton delighted in words and in melodious verse. Even his earliest poems reveal an ear for rhythm and for subtle cadence that lent music also to his mature prose. He was influenced early by the lyric verse of such poets as Robert Louis Stevenson, A.E. Housman, and Rupert Brooke. In January 1922, just turned nineteen, he wrote to his fellow student, Reg Pearse: "I have studied modern poetry fairly carefully, and I find that the trend is more and more to write things which are purely beautiful, not things sensible or deep." A number of his early poems are apparent fruits of a desire to write "[s]ongs that had no meaning but their song". They include, for example, the sonnet beginning, "Far out the waves are calling, Marguerite;/ And listlessly they wander to and fro", and 'Gemellia': "Once in the long dark hours of sleeping/ I woke, and the dawn-wind spoke to me..."

But the ideal of poetry as pure music is possible only in a perfect world — a Garden of Eden. Outside of Eden, in the journey of life, "the deep notes and the undertones" keep intruding, as they do to a greater or less degree in other masters he chose to learn from — Walter de la Mare, Thomas Hardy, and, for dramatic monologues, Robert Browning.

But it was a somewhat lesser poet, Robert Louis Stevenson, who first sounded for Paton a poetic chord that was long to resonate in his own work. As a boy, Paton responded with great emotional intensity to the beauty of the natural world: "I cannot describe my early response to the beauty of hill and stream and tree as anything less than an ecstasy," he says in *Towards the Mountain*; and he adds: "Robert Louis Stevenson expressed my deepest feeelings in those lines from his poem, 'To S.R. Crockett':

> Be it granted to me to behold you again in dying,
> Hills of Home! and to hear again the call;
> Hear about the graves of the martyrs the peewees crying,
> And hear no more at all."

Echoes from this poem, with its elegiac longing for the "Hills of Home", abound in Paton's early poetry. They may be heard, for example, in the poem beginning, "When the last sleep comes, lay me to rest/ Among the green rolling hills I know". They may also be heard in "The grass-larks' call from the open veld/ From Kununata the grey doves call"; and in the several elegies to soldiers fallen in the Boer War. One of these is 'Ladysmith', written at age eighteen, of which the sixth and final quatrain reads:

> Art lonely, son? the moon will pale,
> And o'er the hills come Dawn for thee,
> See, son, these wild veld-flowers I take,
> And twine them on the cross of thee.

Fifty years later he again offered wild veld-flowers in his elegy 'Flowers for the Departed', memorializing four students protesting the Vietnam War who were killed by National Guard gunfire at Kent State University, Ohio, in 1971. By then, Stevenson's voice had faded from his work to be replaced by the deeper tones of Walt Whitman.

QUITE frequently, in the work of a creative writer certain recurring themes and images bespeak a steady inner vision. In Paton's work one such recurring theme has twofold significance: the theme of longing for home. At the simplest level the longing is backward-looking, regretting the loss of a childhood Eden; at another level the longing is forward-looking, relying on a hope for perfection — without evil or suffering — beyond time. Between lies "the journey of the heart". A few lines from the poem 'Meditation for a Young Boy Confirmed', to be found in this volume, encapsulate the entire journey in which, with maturity, Eden must be left behind and the pilgrim journey undertaken:

> Pass over the slender bridges, pick your road quickly through the
> marshes,
> Observe the frail planks left by your predecessors, the stones gained
> only by leaping;
> Press on to the higher ground, to the great hills and the mountains
> From whose heights men survey the eternal country, and the city
> that has no need of moon or sun.
> But do not lie to yourself, admit this is the journey of the heart.

(stanza VII)

This "journey of the heart" informs Paton's biographies of Jan Hofmeyr and Archbishop Clayton; both of them persons of deep Christian faith. It also informs his autobiographies, *Towards the Mountain* and *Journey Continued*, the titles of which allude to Isaiah's vision of the Holy Mountain where the lion lies down at peace with the lamb. His own final estimate of *Cry, the Beloved Country* has similar implications: "It is a song of love for one's own distant country, it is informed with a longing for the land where they shall not hurt or destroy in all that holy mountain." Even his political position rests, ultimately, on his Christian belief in that vision. That is why he could characterize any attempt at theological justification of apartheid as "a Christian heresy"; and it is also why he could accept with equanimity the riposte of his Liberal Party colleague, Hans Meidner: "The trouble with you, Paton, is that you think the Liberal Party is a church." It need not be surprising, therefore, to find that "the journey of the heart" informs Paton's poems, and gives a measure of justification to the classification of the subdivisions of this book as "Journeys".

This volume, *Songs of Africa*, in which Anne Paton has brought together her late husband's verse, including fragments and unfinished pieces, offers a fresh perspective — through the prism of his poetry — on Paton's accomplishment as a writer. Many of the poems reveal a marked gift for lyric verse in the manner of poets he would have read in youth. They also reveal a wide range of other poetic interests, including humorous and recreational verse, satirical verse, dramatic verse in the form of monologues, and religious verse in such diverse forms as psalms, meditations, and prayers. Even the fragments and unfinished pieces play a part by offering testimony to lost creativity through failure of inspiration,

xxiv

personal frustration, or the pressure of the times. Apart from his comparatively unburdened undergraduate days at Natal University College when his muse seemed prolific, Paton's is a sparse harvest of verse, garnered mostly during two brief flowerings of poetic creativity. One of these occupied a span of five months in the second half of 1948 when he first lived in Anerley on the Natal coast after retiring as Principal of Diepkloof Reformatory. The other was the two months or so he spent alone in an isolated forest resort in northern California at the end of 1949.

IN 1935 Paton put aside the literary work of his Pietermaritzburg years to immerse himself in his work of penal reform at Diepkloof Reformatory. It was in the course of a leave of absence from that work to study penal institutions in Europe and North America that the creative urge again came upon him. In Trondheim, following a train journey through an unfamiliar landscape of mountains, streams and pine forests, he was powerfully seized by a longing for home and composed the lyric opening of *Cry, the Beloved Country*: "There is a lovely road that runs from Ixopo into the hills ..." The success of this novel brought him a source of independent income that made it feasible for him to choose retirement from government service in 1948, at age forty-five, rather than face the prospect of the dismantlement of his work at Diepkloof under the hostile administration of Dr. Hendrik Verwoerd. He and his wife moved to Anerley on the Natal south coast where he hoped to settle down as a writer. Paton spent the first weeks of August 1948 reading the works of the American poet Walt Whitman, whose public themes and resonant voice attracted him. By late October he informed his friend, Reg Pearse, that he had written twenty pieces of verse and hoped to publish them soon: "They are not poetry," he wrote, "but deal with the problems of our country. Something gets itself said, and I have to be satisfied with that." The twenty poems he refers to are mostly lyrical pieces of South African provenance, and are probably among the "songs of Africa" he refers to in his poem, 'To Walt Whitman'. They include some of his more successful lyric pieces: 'Sanna', 'The Discardment', 'Dancing Boy', 'Indian Woman' and 'To a Small Boy Who Died at Diepkloof Reformatory'. They also include the ballad in three voices, 'Maria Lee', and the sharp satire on the framers of apartheid: 'We Mean Nothing Evil Towards You'.

Three of these Anerley poems appear to be distilled from Whitman's poem: 'Out of the Cradle Endlessly Rocking'. These are: 'Only the Child is No More', 'Singer of Childhood' and 'To Walt Whitman', which begins:

> Barefooted boy on Paumanok's shore,
> I, not a boy any longer,
> I, having waited longer than you,
> Being a man now, dare not wait any longer,
> For in me too there are a thousand songs,
> And some more sorrowful than yours.

The phrases "on Paumanok's shore" and "more sorrowful than yours" come directly from 'Out of the Cradle' where Whitman recalls a childhood summer on the Long Island shore when, as a lonely, barefoot boy, he observed two mocking-birds nesting. (Paumonok is an Indian name for Long Island.) One day when the female fails to return, her mate laments her in a sustained "song of the heart's outpouring." Whitman composes, in words, the song of the bereft bird. Then, in his own voice, he promises "a thousand songs ... more sorrowful than yours" in return for the childhood wonder the bird's song had re-awakened in the man: "Now in a moment I know what I am for, I awake." Paton's 'To Walt Whitman' also promises a fresh start. It says of "[r]esolutions, plans, programmes and crusades" that:

> All these a time are ended, go and sing.
> And he, astonished, scarcely believing, cried
> What shall I sing? And this voice said, sing
> What else but Africa, songs of Africa,
> The thousand sorrowful songs?

Of Paton's other poems related to 'Out of the Cradle' by the common device of a man looking back on his childhood, the short poem, 'Only the Child is No More', is the least derivative and the most perfect. By contrast, the longer and more ambitious poem, 'Singer of Childhood', addressed to a rainbird, is more derivative and less successful. It is of interest, nevertheless, for in it Paton translates a theme from Whitman to an African setting to declare the river of childhood past, and the songs of Africa beckoning:

> Singer of childhood, there shall never be captured now
> The song that your forerunner sang to the child.
> For age has corrupted it, the deep notes sound deeper
> The sorrowful more sorrowful, the deepest concluding.

Tell me no longer of the well-loved river
Of childhood, but intone to me Africa
The whole continent of rivers and streams
And its thousand sorrowful songs.

'Singer of Childhood', although included in this volume, seems to be an unfinished work. (The lines just quoted may be an earlier version of the lines quoted above from 'To Walt Whitman'.) Apart from a revised extract in German translation, Paton did not publish it.

It is no wonder Paton invoked Whitman when setting out to write poems that would "deal with the problems of our country." He would certainly have appreciated Whitman's emotional intensity and sonorous music, for Whitman was at heart a rhapsodist, and Paton was inclined to be one too. He would have found Whitman's rhythms congenial because they evoke, as do passages in Paton's prose, a memory of the cadences and repetition of Hebrew poetry that survive in Bible translations. He may also have had a strong sense of kinship with Whitman. They shared a reverent awe before nature. They also shared a great capacity for compassion, and a firm dedication to human freedom. Whitman brought these qualities of mind and heart to the struggle against slavery, and subsequently to his years of voluntary care for the wounded of America's bloody Civil War; and Paton brought them, first to his work as a penal reformer, then to the writing of his novels, and, later, to his years of service to the Liberal Party in opposition to apartheid in South Africa. Both men also shared an extraordinary regard for Abraham Lincoln. Paton speaks of Lincoln in his autobiography as "one of the greatest men of history, surely the greatest of all the rulers of nations"; and he places Lincoln among some exalted company in his poem, 'Meditation For a Young Boy Confirmed': "Do not pronounce judgment on the Infinite, nor suppose God to be like a bad Prime Minister .... He is not greater than Plato or Lincoln, nor superior to Shakespeare and Beethoven, He is their God." Whitman's reverence for Lincoln has its great outpouring in the elegy, 'When Lilacs Last in the Dooryard Bloom'd' — a poem that Paton could hardly find words laudatory enough to describe. He spoke of it as: "[o]ne of the greatest threnodies in the language", and he incorporates lines from it into his elegy on the students killed at Kent State University in 1971, 'Flowers for the Departed', and into his memorial for his first wife, *Kontakion for You Departed*. It was fitting that the new voice to be heard in the "Songs of Africa" of 1948 should be prefaced by a dedication to Whitman.

ON December 4, 1948, Paton's friend and mentor, and former Deputy Prime Minister, Jan H. Hofmeyr, died; and with him died Paton's hopes for a strong parliamentary opposition to the implementation of apartheid. He did not involve himself directly in politics in the immediate aftermath of Hofmeyr's death. He had just embarked on life as a professional writer. He travelled extensively during 1949 — in South Africa, England and America — because of his involvement with the filming of *Cry, the Beloved Country* and with rehearsals for *Lost in the Stars*, a musical by Maxwell Anderson and Kurt Weill based on the novel. In October 1949 his wife, Dorrie, joined him in New York for the Broadway opening, and afterwards they went to northern California to visit Aubrey Burns and his wife who, three years before, had first read *Cry, the Beloved Country* and recommended its publication. Dorrie Paton returned home in mid-November for the confirmation of their younger son, thirteen year old Jonathan. Paton, who admired the great California redwood trees with an almost religious awe, began a solitary stay at Lane's Flat Cabins, an otherwise deserted redwood forest resort — a place even more distant and different from his home than Trondheim, Norway, where loneliness had inspired the lyrical opening of *Cry, the Beloved Country*. In that solitary place he hoped to write a novel of Christ's appearance in Johannesburg. (The poem 'No Place for Adoration' touches on its theme.) While there he read "daily portions of St. Mark's gospel, Robert Frost, Thoreau's *Walden* ... and a good deal of Whitman." But his novel did not satisfy him, and he abandoned the project after several chapters.

While his two month stay at Lane's Flat produced no novel, it did produce a harvest of verse comparable to that of the early months at Anerley the year before but generally more religious in tone. Among other things, he wrote a number of psalms and, possibly, the long allegory, 'I Came To a Valley'. At the Christmas season, with his family far distant, he was very homesick; which homesickness, he says, was to have a consequence like that of Trondheim: "not quite so spectacular; but just as real." In the early hours of January 4, 1950, "under the influence of strong emotion," he wrote 'Meditation for a Young Boy Confirmed', a poem marking the confirmation of his son, Jonathan. This poem — in long cadenced lines — is the most sustained and the most fully realized of his works in verse; and it could be described, as Paton described *Cry, the Beloved Country*, as "informed with longing for that land where they shall not hurt or destroy in all that holy mountain." More particularly, as the lines quoted earlier illustrate, it is a spiritual *aide-memoire* for a young person leaving the innocent Eden of childhood and setting foot on the

Pilgrim Way. The 'Meditation' attracted greater attention than any other poem of Paton's. It was first printed in *The Christian Century* (1954) and later in *Theology* (1959); and it was issued separately in London by the Society For Promoting Christian Knowledge in 1959.

During the era of his work for the Liberal Party, Paton's creative urge had to be diverted to the writing of pamphlets like *The People Wept* and *The Charlestown Story*; the series of political columns, *The Long View*; and political oratory — much of it memorable; as, for example, his address of July 12, 1956, to the annual congress of the Liberal Party, 'Beware of Melancholy'. His poems of that period, such as 'Praise Song for Luthuli', are, therefore, infrequent, and mostly occasional. In the period following 1968, when the Liberal Party was legislated out of existence, his poems remain infrequent and the circumstances that occasion them are apt to be sombre, as for instance 'Death of a Priest', 'Caprivi Lament' and 'Necklace of Fire'.

The last piece of writing of his life confirms Paton's love of the spoken word in poem or oration. The editors of *Time* commissioned an article on the state of affairs in South Africa; but he composed instead an encomium on the spoken arts. Among "great orators" of his lifetime he names Winston Churchill, Reinhold Niebuhr (the American theologian), his own friend, J.H. Hofmeyr, and General J.C. Smuts. He is lavish in his praise of poems he loved including Yeats' 'The Fiddler of Dooney', Blake's 'The Tyger', and Francis Thompson's 'The Hound of Heaven'. (His own poem, 'The Prison House', bears some resemblance to Thompson's.) He pays special homage to Psalm 139 and to Whitman's 'When Lilacs Last in the Dooryard Bloom'd': "one of the most memorable tributes paid by any human being to another." Of his own work he says: "My creative and literary imagination will never again rise to any great height"; and he supplies two examples of what he could no longer achieve in words. His first is a passage from *Cry, the Beloved Country* beginning: "The great red hills stand desolate, and the earth has torn away like flesh." As his second example he quotes the final lines of 'To a Small Boy Who Died at Diepkloof Reformatory', including a line on the home-bound soul — "Fly home-bound soul to the great Judge-President" — that might aptly apply to his own going home:

> So do I commit you,
> Your frail body to the waiting ground,
> Your dust to the dust of the veld, —
> Fly home-bound soul to the great Judge-President
> Who unencumbered by the pressing need
> To give society protection, may pass on you
> The sentence of indeterminate compassion.

©Edward Callan 1995

Alan S. Paton (centre) with Reginald O. Pearse (left) and Cyril Armitage (right) — Natal University College 1921

ALAN PATON: A CHRONOLOGY

Born: Alan Stewart Paton, 11 January 1903, Pietermaritzburg, Natal

Educated: Maritzburg College (1914-1918)
Natal University College (BSc and Diploma in Education, 1919-1924). Graduates with distinction in physics.

1920: Publishes his first poem 'To a Picture' in *Natal University College* Magazine.

1925-28: Ixopo High School (teaching mathematics and chemistry)

1927: Friendship with J.H. Hofmeyr begins.

1928: Marries Doris Olive Francis at Ixopo.

1928-35: Moves to Pietermaritzburg, to teach at Maritzburg College.

1930: David Paton born.
Joins South African Institute of Race Relations.

1934: Spends three months recuperating at Park Rynie from enteric (typhoid) fever.

1935: Appointed Principal of Diepkloof Reformatory (for African boys) in Johannesburg.

1936: Jonathan Paton born.

1942: Nominated to the Anglican Diocesan Commission to inquire into church and race relationships in South Africa.

1946: Studies penal institutions in Europe, the United States and Canada, and writes *Cry, the Beloved Country* while travelling.

1948: Publishes *Cry, the Beloved Country*
The National Party comes to power
Resigns from Diepkloof Reformatory, to live and write at Anerley on the Natal South Coast.

1949: Visits the United States for the opening of *Lost in the Stars*, a musical based on *Cry, the Beloved Country*.

Spends two months at Lane's Flat Cabins near Piercy, California.

1950: Spends two months in London, working on the film script of *Cry, the Beloved Country*.

1953: Moves to Botha's Hill to work on a Tuberculosis (TB) settlement.
Publishes *Too Late the Phalarope*.

1954: Tours the United States to write on race relations for *Colliers'*.
Leaves TB settlement.

1954-68: Chairman, later National President of the Liberal Party of South Africa until the party, being multiracial, was forced to disband under the Prohibition of Interference Act.

1955: Spends two months, on the invitation from Father John Patterson, teaching at Kent School, Connecticut.

1957: Completes script for *Mkhumbane* (Village in the Gully) based on life in the township of Cato Manor, Durban.

1960: Opening of *Mkhumbane*, with music by Todd Matshikiza, performed Durban 29 March, and directed by Malcolm Woolfson.
State of Emergency declared by the South African government 30 March
Passport confiscated on return from America

1967: Death of Doris Paton

1968: Publishes *Instrument of Thy Peace*.

1969: Marries Anne Margaret Hopkins and moves from Kloof to Botha's Hill.

1970: Passport returned.

1975: Publishes *Knocking on the Door: Shorter Writings* (edited by Colin Gardner).

1980 : Publishes *Towards the Mountain* — first volume of his autobiography.

1981: Publishes third novel *Ah, but your Land is Beautiful*.

1988: 12 April, dies at Lintrose, Botha's Hill, Natal.
November: *Journey Continued* — second volume of his autobiography — published.

Songs of Africa

FIRST JOURNEY

BEGINNINGS

EARLY IMPRESSIONS

To a Picture

He gazes on me with his long-dead eyes,
And dumbly strives to tell me how he died,
And shows the hilt-stabbed dagger in his side;
I see mad terror there; the murd'rous cries
Draw near — more near — half-tottering he tries
To reach the door — one step! — "unbar, 'tis I."
But none unbar — I hear the broken cry,
I see the mirrored anguish in his eyes.
So conjure I the tale; the faded print
Hangs on the bedroom wall, and there I see
Those wild eyes ever gazing on my bed.
They lead me to strange wonderings; what hint,
What sign, what tragic muteness will there be
In mine own eyes, when they do find me dead?

Signed "Ubi"; probably Paton's first published poem
Natal University College Magazine, November 1920

(See Notes at the end for further references to the various poems)

2

The Sea

Distant mumbling . . .
Distant rumbling . . . of the sea!
Just a murmur, till the wind
Comes up shrilling from behind
The sandy dunes; then it grows,
Ever growing as it blows,
Till it rushes into one majestic boom,
Like the long, resounding, thundering of Doom!

Then the whining of the wind dies away . . .
All is silent with the silence of the grave;
Hushed and muffled is the rumbling mumble save
For the echo as it echoes, in the hollow, down the dunes.

Racing inwards are the billows of the sea,
And one rears its lofty head above the rest,
Diamonds flashing from its proud and haughty crest,
Racing inwards, flinging droplets o'er the yest,
Merrily.

Sweeping nearer to that endless stretch of brown,
And its crest to meet the rocky surf curls o'er,
And it crashes and it thunders on the shore,
With a hollow, dull, reverberating roar,
Cruelly.

Swirling upwards are the billows of the sea,
And the frothing, foaming onrush surges o'er
The dogged, rugged ramparts on the shore,
The rocks that beetle there for evermore,
Eternally.

Spreading shorewards are the billows of the sea,
And seething swish they softly o'er the sand,
The receding wash the bosom of the land,
Swilling sea-shells as they nestle on the strand,
Tenderly.

Yet they're treach'rous, are the billows of the sea,
They are cold and grim and cruel, under night's black, driving
    skies,
As savagely they ravage at the rampart that defies,
With a cold and cruel crooning o'er the wretch who by them
    dies,
Miserably.

And involunt'ry I shudder, for it fills me with affright,
Does the ocean's lonely grandeur, on this moonless, starless
    night,
And I turn my footsteps homewards, past the looming, ghostly
    dunes,
Till I can but hear the mumbling, distant rumbling of the sea,
And it seems as tho' a burden has been lifted off from me.

Just murmur, till the wind
Comes up shrilling from behind
The sandy dunes; then it grows,
Ever growing as it blows,
Till it rushes into one majestic boom
Like the long, resounding, thundering of doom!

Then the whining of the wind dies away . . .
All is silent with the silence of the grave;
Hushed and muffled is the rumbling mumble save
For the echo, as it echoes, in the hollow, down the dunes.

Signed L.T.
Natal University College Magazine, 1921

4

Sonnet — To Sleep

There is a joy in dossing in a tent,
    More than in anything that e'er was made,
    Although the blankets are all marmalade,
And though one wonders where the chocolate went;
Here friendship finds its highest, fullest vent,
    As hand-in-hand through realms of milk we wade,
    And sleep on butter of the highest grade,
And breathe in eager draughts the healthy scent
Of meat that has long seen the prime of youth.
Here apricot and eggs our forms embrace,
And make jam omelettes around my leg,
Which may be sad, but 'tis, I swear, the truth.
Here lonely sardines do our friendship beg,
And in the night we meet them face to face.

Signed O.F.
Natal University College Magazine, 1922

Song of the Northward-Bound

I sing the song of the Northward-bound
    As she swings on the Northward trail.
I sing the song that is sung by the sound
    Of the wheels on the gleaming rail.

I sing the song of the hurrying wheels
    As she thunders round the bend,
As they beat their sharp tattoo on the steels
    That lead to the journey's end.

The earth below me throbs and quakes,
And through the trees there stirs and breaks
    The headlights' blinding stream.
The cutting sides are bright as day
As the mail roars on her Northward way
    In fire and smoke and steam.

At night when the valleys darken
    And dark are the hills around,
I lie in my bed and I hearken
    For the call of the Northward-bound.

From the far domain of the dreaming shores
    As they sleep by the moonlit sea,
Through the heavy mists of the night she roars
    And calls in the night to me.

And the sleeping river starts and wakes
    And shrinks from the blinding light.
And the mighty framework reels and shakes,
While the Northbound call sounds over all,
    As she dies away in the night.

Round the curves she rattles and swerves
    In the hills of the thorn-tree belt.
I have cried for joy at her string of lights
And her call that cheers a man o' nights
    In the uttermost parts of the veld.

Aye, oft in the hills of the thorn-tree belt
    I have heard the Northbound call.
But where they sleep on the lonely veld
    It sounds the saddest of all.

Dark, and a wind that rustles by me
    In the mist of a weary rain.
Dark, and the dead that sleep by me
    In the sleep of Colenso plain.

Light, and a thunder of wheels with the light,
    And a deafening tumult of sound,
That as sudden dies away in the night,
Till silence and darkness are over all,
And ever the mist and the sad rain fall,
Yet hark, there sounds the saddest of all,
    The call of the Northward bound.

Natal University College Magazine, 1922

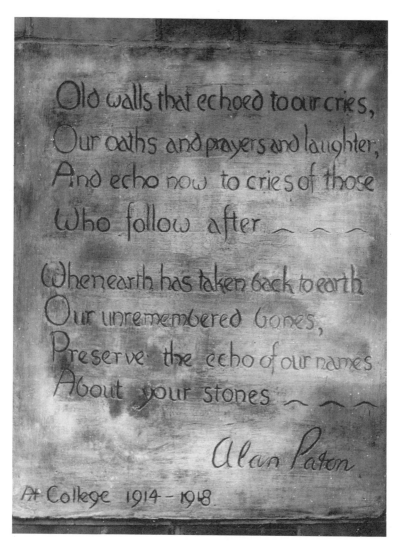

Old walls that echoed to our cries,
Our oaths and prayers and laughter,
And echo now to cries of those
Who follow after ~ ~ ~

When earth has taken back to earth
Our unremembered bones,
Preserve the echo of our names
About your stones ~ ~ ~

Alan Paton

At College 1914 - 1918

*In 1963, Paton was asked to inscribe these words on the southern
wall of the Maritzburg College gymnasium*

8

COLLEGE POEMS

Old walls . . .

Old walls that echoed to our cries,
Our oaths and prayers and laughter,
And echo now to cries of those
Who follow after.

When earth has taken back to earth
Our unremembered bones,
Preserve the echo of our names
About your stones.

Written in 1928, but untitled
Maritzburg College Magazine, 1934

School

For unpermitted tramp of naked feet,
For rank purloinment of their neighbours' goods,
For wicked upturned barb on master's seat,
For bloody warfare in forbidden woods,
For spectral use of sacred Gov'ment sheets,
For fierce disputed ownership of knives,
For high imaginative boast of sire's feats,
For quick-repented robbery of hives.
For midnight's surreptitious food and drink,
For twin empurpled eyes to right the wrong,
For foully murdered learning, mourned in ink,
For new apparel bartered for a son,
I yearn, to feel beneath my hands again,
The master hands that Thou has given me,
To mould, and fashion, and yield back to Thee,
Alive with love and laughter, Thine own men.

Pietermaritzburg, 28 October 1928
Unpublished

10

Trilemma

I dreamt three students walked a road
Nobly degreed and capped and gowned;
A humble labourer in a field
Close on the roadside tilled the ground.

One student wrapped in lofty thought
Passed by with neither sight nor sign.
I saw his face beneath the hood
And gaped bewildered — it was mine!

One student smelt the honest sweat,
Screwed up his nose in cold disdain.
I saw his face beneath the hood,
Gaped more bewildered — mine again!

One student leapt the roadside hedge
And tilled the ground without a word
Beside his mate — I saw his face,
This dream was growing more absurd!

But most absurd of all was me,
The real me, not the other three,
Going from hood to hood to see
Which of the three was really me!

Pietermaritzburg, 3 April 1932
Natal University College Magazine, 1932

Memories 1919-1924

With many very brilliant men
    I was at N.U.C.
But oh! alas, the most of them
    Have far outdistanced me.

There's Adolf, he's quite famous now,
    And figures in "Who's Who."
And woe to him who does the things
    That Adolf used to do.

And Freddie's word in tennis worlds
    Carries some weight, I hear.
Though nothing like the weight that his
    Poor motorbike must bear.

Young Nuttall's at the D.H.S.
    The Head's right hand, you know.
I give this as a certain fact,
    For Nuttall told me so.

Young Richardson has won the Rhodes,
    The news quite staggered me.
In fairness though, the Rhodes has gone
    To queerer birds than he.

Old Mooney sits in some small lane,
    Some office three by four.
And — well, he knows the libel laws,
    I'll not say any more.

Dear Dr. Bronstein's settled down
    In quarters fit for kings,
Where he will rise on our dead selves
    To far, far better things.

And I? I teach, and try to build
The new Jerusalem,
One's progress gets a check or two,
But one can't notice them.

Natal University College Magazine, 1929

POEMS OF SETTLEMENT AND HISTORY

Ladysmith
(Midnight on the Battlefields)

Art lonely, son? see, the pale moon
Sheds holy radiance over thee;
The veld-grass rustles in the wind,
And Mother Veld doth mother thee.

Art lonely, son? the sight of this,
The last, sad resting-place of thee,
Hath stirred what e'er of soul I have,
I, prayerless, breathe a prayer for thee.

Art lonely, son? the whole, wide world
Is known to me, yet this of thee
Hath done what never world could do,
I, dry-eyed, weep hot tears for thee.

Art lonely, son? there in the church
Is thy dear mother's gift to thee;
Thy grave unseen, she joys; the veld,
Her sister-mother, mothers thee.

Art lonely, son? e'en I must go,
And leave the loneliness to thee,
For my own mother waits afar,
And she too, son, shall know of thee.

Art lonely, son? the moon will pale,
And o'er the hills come Dawn for thee,
See, son, these wild veld-flowers I take,
And twine them on the cross of thee.

Ladysmith, 13 July 1921
Natal University College Magazine, 1921

14

The grass-larks' call . . .

The grass-larks' call from the open veld
From Kununata the grey doves call,
But the sound of his voice, the tramp of his feet,
Shall be heard no more at all.

The skirl of the pipes in last lament
Has followed him to his place of sleep,
His eyes shall not see the beloved hills
Nor men that plough and plant and reap.

The valley of death is sounded for him,
The leaves of the oak fall soft on his face,
We leave him at last, soldier and friend,
To silence and rest and the peace of the place.

The sun will sink in the red of the west,
Around him his hills will grow quiet and dim,
From Kununata the doves will mourn
And the larks will call in the veld for him.

Ixopo, 21 December 1929
Unpublished and untitled

15

Maritzburg in February

The sun goes trailing pitiless
A ball of fire on azure ground,
And drags the earth's unwilling hand
Upon its lifeless round.

Men gasp the air in dizzy streets
And curse the sun, the sky, the drought,
The pavement stones lie half-alive,
Their tongues are hanging out.

The clock sounds flatly from the tower,
At twelve, its strength is nearly spent,
The bronzéd faces shine with sweat
Up on the monument.

The trams when weary quarters strike
Go listless to their work again,
Into the gutters asphalt streets
Weep tears of bitumen.

Come leave the heavy-lidded haze
To where the burning cannas grow,
And watch them in a sea of fire
Go dancing to and fro.

Their red and bronze battalions shout
A truceless challenge to the sun,
When weaker brethren prostrate lie
They revel in the fun.

Day-long the cricket cheers them on,
And when the beaten sun has fled,
They light their comrade in the dark
Up fairy stairs to bed.

Natal University College Magazine, 1932

The farmers know . . .

The farmers know the peace of God
They read the riddle of the sod
And ponder not on death or birth.

I where the shadows of the clouds
Over the fields go fleeing
Am brought to muse on cents and pounds
And the mystery of being.

They when they've followed with slow tread
Some comrade to his resting place
Go leaving dead to talk with dead
And raise their eyes from his last bed
To look for tears on the sky's face.

And I am left with the funeral dove
And the wind that sighs in the funeral trees
We change no word in the solemn place
For his eyes are on the sky above
He speaks no word of mysteries
But looks for tears on the sky's face.

Lodesborough, 21 January 1934
Unpublished and untitled

SECOND JOURNEY

AWAKENING

POEMS OF DESIRE AND REDEMPTION

You and I —

You and I —
Ah! what care I?
Let the whole world die,
Let the leaves fade,
And all that's made,
Wither and die.
Let the birds not fly;
Let the sky be blue,
Or the sky be grey,
Or any such hue
Adorn the sky.
For what care I,
When I have you?

The world did not die,
The leaves did not fade,
And all that was made,
Did not wither and die.
But the cruel sky
Had no hue.
It was black as Death,
And fled was the breath
Of you.

Then the world died,
And the leaves did fade,
And all that was made
Withered and died.
The rivers dried
By the green bank-side,
And the banks grew brown,

And the leaves fell down,
And the boughs stood bare,
And the birds of the air,
Fell and died.
The ocean moaned,
And the tempest's roar
From the howling shore
Was tortured and wild,
The broken cry
Of one without child.
And I thought of the days
When my heart was young,
Of the foolish song
That a fool had sung.
"Let the slow bells toll,
And the slow knells roll,
Let them bury the dead,
When their breath is fled.
For what care I
If the whole world die?"
And the slow bells tolled,
And the slow knells rolled,
And they buried the dead,
When her breath was fled.
God! hark to the cry
Of my tortured soul:
"Let me die!"
But no bells toll,
And no knells roll,
For aye.

The Eisteddfod Poetry Book, 1921

(See Notes at the end for further references to the various poems)

Sonnet

I

Far out the waves are calling, Marguerite;
    And listlessly they wander to and fro,
    Disconsolate, as if they did not know
What keeps you from their music, wild and sweet.
I hear the pattering of little feet
    That earnestly are seeking there below;
    They call your name so loving as they go,
How can I ever tell them, Marguerite?
Now life and joy is over, Marguerite,
And I must live for ever in the dark,
You will forgive me if I do not show
A deep unutterable hate; for hark,
I hear them call as if they did not know,
How can I hate them for it, Marguerite?

Natal University College Magazine, 1922

To —

Ah! why do you come in the hours of dark,
And hold out your arms at the window there,
And your face is so sad and so wondrous fair,
And you speak so low and so pleadingly
The sacred words that were all to me
In the days that are long passed by?

Ah! why do you come in the hours of dark,
And look with those eyes and their unshed tears?
Do you not know that the wounds of years
Will break anew if the word is said?
Do you not know tho' your love is dead,
That mine can never die?

Is it kind to come in the hours of dark?
When healing sleep calms the turbulent mind,
I suddenly wake with a start and find
Your pleading arms and your pleading eyes,
And your pleading voice as it brokenly dies
In the midst of its mute appeal.

Is it kind to come in the hours of dark?
To part wide the lips I often have kissed,
To call with the voice I could never resist
I will come, for 'tis you — whether cruel or kind —
I will come as before — as before I will find
You have left me naught but the mocking wind,
And wounds that never will heal.

Signed N.B.
Natal University College Magazine, 1923

23

Gemellia

Once in the long dark hours of sleeping
    I woke, and the dawn-wind spoke to me,
And told me there was a woman weeping
    Down in the pines by the sea.

So I went to the pines in the dawn-wind's blowing
    Coldly and keenly over the sea,
Pale in the East, and long hair flowing,
    Gemellia passed by me.

And I, I turned and followed after
    With throbbing heart and soul in me,
But there was naught but mocking laughter
    Over the misty sea.

And now each morn in the dawn-wind's blowing
    Cold and keen in the pines by the sea,
Pale in the East, and long hair flowing,
    Gemellia passes by me.

And now each morn I follow after
    With that same mad heart and soul in me,
But there is never aught but that mocking laughter
    Over the misty sea.

Natal University College Magazine, 1924

Sister Street

Red dawn is in the desert
And the wind is warm and sweet,
And the warm wind of the desert
It blows in Sister Street.

I hear the sound of voices
And the sound of many feet,
And they are for ever passing
Down in Sister Street.

Wine and mirth and laughter,
Wine and laughter and mirth,
And a song or two thereafter,
The saddest songs of earth.

The desert wind is warm and sweet
And the desert dawn is red,
And I feel it blow in Sister Street
When the skies are grey as lead.

There are weary eyes that close there
O so wearily,
And Wearier Eyes that watch there,
The Weariest Eyes that be.

Sister Street, Sister Street,
Laughter and song and mirth,
I feel it blow in Sister Street,
The saddest street of earth.

Natal University College Magazine, 1925

The Prostitute

With man's first disobedience and the fall
Fate caring not for evil or for good
Carved out a niche eternal for your place,
With you for wares, the pavement for your stall,
And as a lure for quickening men's blood
Inviting eyes set in a painted face.

Kings were your custom, prophets and holy priests,
Soldiers, scholars, monks and beardless boys,
Husbands of loving wives, respected sires,
Muffling their heads in cloaks, hungry as beasts.
Some brooded stoney-eyed after your joys,
Over the ashes cold of their dead fires.

Vows made to God were broken by your eyes,
Things taught to stripling sons gone all forgot.
With hammering temples man is stripped and stark
With hot desire to clutch the thing he buys.
This vile thing is, and other things are not
For those poor souls who traffic in the dark.

Your lips are scarlet with the blood of men,
Your trophies are their lost virginities,
Your arms beasts rampant on a painted face.
Some scaled with vice, and they will come again,
Some fine of soul, haunted by memories
That will not leave them, of your one embrace.

Your eyes are heavy-lidded mystery,
They mock, or drop demure, or fill with tears
To make a eunuch dream of dead delight.
What matter if some boy ere he can flee
Sees the sweet building of the dogged years
To earth go crashing in one tragic night?

Yet what if some recount your tale of sin,
Cast pious glance to heaven as you go by,
Then chase you with afraid but lecherous eyes,
Finding the woman more than Magdalen?
What is their judgement by your own dumb cry
That nothing have at all but what man buys?

What have you now, poor sister of the street?
Children perhaps, with neither sire nor name,
Daughters perhaps, on the same errand sped
On younger, prettier, more successful feet.
And their foul nemesis shall be the same
Dread legacy of Mediterranean dead.

Pietermaritzburg, 16 February 1931
Unpublished

Scottsville, 1931

Where with his heavy-swinging trunk
The elephant went up and down,
The lights are strung along his track
And trams go thro' the pavéd town.

Last night a woman ran to me
And sobbing caught me by the arm,
Gone frantic with the age-old fear
That she might come to woman's harm.

I saw no soul, I heard no sound,
But knew that in some modern man
Under the lights of town, the old
Primordial savage stirred again.

Pietermaritzburg, 13 March 1931
Natal University College Magazine, 1931

27

Poor Whites

They leave the ploughshare and the sod.
Their shiftless feet in veldskoen shod
Drag in the alien street
That many a path more sweet
Have trod.

The jackal prowling thro' the tares
Of starlight fields that once were theirs,
He knows no fret of bars,
His limits are the stars,
He has no cares.

When body hungers with desire
His call will waken answering fire,
And some as-hungry mate
Will answer him and wait
For him to sire.

The ox that dumbly draws the load
Along the sweet and lonely road,
He has the dark for friend
And at his journey's end
A safe abode.

Of passion is his body shorn
As virginal as he was born,
Who knows but half-ashamed
It surges mute and maimed
And sinks forlorn?

And in their slattern veldskoen shod
That many a sweeter path have trod,
Their women walk the street
And sell for bread and meat
The gift of God.

Natal University College Magazine, 1931

28

The Prodigals

Out of our fathers' land in former years
We marched, hating their rites, their narrow ways;
We left in high revolt, nor love nor tears
Could turn us from our purpose in those days.

For us no valley of iniquity
Where men went hungry for the sin of birth,
We cursed their God, and their hypocrisy,
And left to build a better place on earth.

But now 'tis otherwise, and as men tire
Of flaming aloe and the stony sand,
Of flowers and of skies that burn like fire,
We turn our aging feet to quiet land.

Leaving the husks of our revolt, we turn,
To valley long unthought-of, weary feet,
Yet in our journey never thought to learn
The rivers of our fathers ran so sweet.

Nor thought to learn that willing we would bind
Tradition's shackles on unwithered limbs,
Nor thought in meek and new amaze to find
Beauty and healing in their ancient hymns.

Yet truth be in our words — 'tis not entire
For peace and comfort that we turn us home;
Out in our desert where our lips afire
Once foamed with truth, do now our children's foam.

They curse our Gods, and with most bestial sin
Foul our dear temples till we cry "let be."
What use to cry? What use of crying in
A world where others cry more loud than we?

Natal University College Magazine, 1933

29

Maria Lee

Hanged September 17, 1948, for the slow murder by arsenic of her
lover. She went to the gallows singing hymns.

The slow marching
The measured marching
The feet marching to the mystery
The woman singing
The last singing
Singing her way to the mystery

    I am the Resurrection
    I am the Life
    The Lord saith
    Whosoever liveth
    And in Me believeth
    Shall taste not of death.

Silence most dread
But for the tread
Of the feet marching to the mystery
But for the singing
The woman singing
Singing her way to the mystery

    Scarce opened the womb
    When opens the tomb
    Scarce forgotten the birth
    When brief as a flower
    Completed his hour
    Man is cut from the earth

I am the Resurrection . . .
But I am the dead
'Tis my feet marching to the mystery
The footfalls of doom
Sound in the gloom
As I march to the room of the mystery.

The dread company
That comes with me
Halts.
No sound
Silence profound
In these vaults.

This is the end
Let me ascend
The steps that lead to the mystery.
Suffer me not
For pains of death
In this last falling to fall from Thee

Hangman, to whom
In this hour of my doom
To whom in this hour
Is given God's power
Hangman, I bow,
Garland me now.

In the gloom stumbling
Drunken stumbling
Feet stumbling from the mystery.
Eyes meet no eyes
Words no replies
Fleeing the room of the mystery.

Is life then so pressing
That forgetting the blessing
You stream through the door?
The grace of our lord
The love of our God
Be with you all evermore.

Anerley, 19 September 1948

Sanna

The village lies in Sabbath heat
The dog lies in the sun
But stern and strict the elders go
They pass me one by one.

The alien traffic swirls and blows
The dust about the street
But stern and strict the elders go
In any dust or heat.

And careless words are spoken
By idlers of the place
But stern and strict the elders go
To hear the words of grace.

And stern and strict the sabbath clothes
And stern the eyes above
And stern and strict the elders go
To hear the words of love.

And Sanna follows all demure
And plays her little part
The child of love moves in her womb
And terror in her heart.

Anerley, 3 February 1949
Knocking on the Door, 1975

The Prison House

I ran from the prison house but they captured me
And he met me there at the door with a face of doom
And motioned me to go to his private room
And he took my rank from me, and gave me the hell
Of his tongue, and ordered me to the runaway cell
With the chains and the walls, and the long night days, and the
    gloom.

And once on leave that goes to the well-behaved
I jumped in fright from the very brothel bed
And through the midnight streets like a mad thing fled
Sobbing with fear lest the door be closed on me
And in silence he let me pass, he let me be,
No word but your clothing's disarranged, he said.

And once in a place where I was, I told a man
Whence I was come, and who was in charge, and he
Said God, but I never thought in my life to see
A man from that place, and I wish to God I was there,
Yes. I wish I was there. So I went back on air
And he smiled at me at the door, he smiled at me.

And once when he drew the blood from my rebel flesh
With foul and magnificent words I cursed and reviled
His name and his house and his works, and drunk with my pain
    and wild
I seized the whip from his hands and slashed him again
And again and again, and made him pay for my pain,
Till I fell at his feet and wept on the stone like a child.

He can take the hide from my back, the sight from my eyes,
The lust of my loins and the sounds of the earth from me,
Fruit's taste, and the scent of the flowers and the salt of the sea,
The thoughts of the mind, and the words of music and fire
That comforted me, so long as he does not require
These chains that now are become as garments to me.

Northampton, 24 September 1949
Instrument of Thy Peace, 1968

33

Sonnet — To Sleep

I

Sleep is the mocking thing when the mind's knot
Won't yield and loosen, when the mind's eye fears
To close completely, when the mind's ear hears
Rumours of danger, plot and counter-plot,
And threats and intrigues, and the long night's shot
All through and through with restlessness and tears
For dreams that steal the savings of the years
And wake one for relief to find it not.
And when I dream that fortune's hand has reft
From me the world's last promise, or the bright
Last chance that's now or never, or the key
To the lost door that was the last door left,
Or wake to reach and touch you in the night
And find you gone, then sleep's the mockery.

II

Sleep is the lovely thing when swift and deep
She takes me down into the halls of night
And draws the blessed blinds upon the bright
Incessant sun. A lovely thing is sleep,
Her constant and caressing fingers steep
The mind in gentleness, smoothe out the tight
Furrows of vigilance, and dreams invite
That only her caressing fingers keep.
She conquers children, makes the naughtiest
Into the likeness of angels, meek
And innocent of any mischieving.
And when I reach my hand and touch your breast
Contented, and you lost in sleeping speak
Contentedly, why sleep's the lovely thing.

Lane's Flat, 6 December 1949
Unpublished

34

The blood poured . . .

The blood poured, bubbling like panthers
That losing their guts through hatred's holes
Drenched old maids' knitting and bespattered
The new born with caryatids
Sanguine and sexless
On a grinning battleship.

Undated: probably Lane's Flat, January 1950
Unpublished and untitled

This love is warm . . .

This love is warm, knowing no artifice
But that of loving, and in passion needs
None of abandon's whips, for that it seeks
Nothing but to be one with what it loves
And it is clean and chaste, seeking no end
But what it loves.

New York, 24 January, 1950
Unpublished and untitled

To a Small Boy Who Died at Diepkloof Reformatory

Small offender, small innocent child
With no conception or comprehension
Of the vast machinery set in motion
By your trivial transgression,
Of the great forces of authority,
Of judges, magistrates, and lawyers,
Psychologists, psychiatrists, and doctors,
Principals, police, and sociologists,
Kept moving and alive by your delinquency,
This day, and under the shining sun
Do I commit your body to the earth
Oh child, oh lost and lonely one.

Clerks are moved to action by your dying;
Your documents, all neatly put together,
Are transferred from the living to the dead,
Here is the document of birth
Saying that you were born and where and when,
But giving no hint of joy or sorrow,
Or if the sun shone, or if the rain was falling,
Or what bird flew singing over the roof
Where your mother travailed. And here your name
Meaning in white man's tongue, he is arrived,
But to what end or purpose is not said.

Here is the last certificate of Death;
Forestalling authority he sets you free,
You that did once arrive have now departed
And are enfolded in the sole embrace
Of kindness that earth ever gave to you.
So negligent in life, in death belatedly
She pours her generous abundance on you
And rains her bounty on the quivering wood
And swaddles you about, where neither hail nor tempest,
Neither wind nor snow nor any heat of sun

Shall now offend you, and the thin cold spears
Of the highveld rain that once so pierced you
In falling on your grave shall press you closer
To the deep repentant heart.

Here is the warrant of committal,
For this offence, oh small and lonely one,
For this offence in whose commission
Millions of men are in complicity
You are committed. So do I commit you,
Your frail body to the waiting ground,
Your dust to the dust of the veld, —
Fly home-bound soul to the great Judge-President
Who unencumbered by the pressing need
To give society protection, may pass on you
The sentence of the indeterminate compassion.

Anerley, March 1949
Knocking on the Door, 1975

TRANSLATIONS AND TRANSITIONS

Sonnet

II

Give me my sword — and gird it on, my son,
    Where, in past days I girded it, and bore
    It o'er my head, dripping and drenched with gore.
Let my old sightless eyes gaze loving on
It's shining steel again — how the sun shone!
    This dint? That was the crest old Gustrum wore,
    Shouting "Hast prayed?" — Old Gustrum prayed no more,
I clove him to the horse he rode upon.
'Tis broken here; some fool lord with a sneer
On his fool face, couched lance and rode on me.
We met and shuddered as two mighty ships
That meet in fog at night in some dark sea.
What sayest thou, son? Poor fool, did'st thou not hear?
    Could my lord sneer, when my lord had no lips?

Natal University College Magazine, 1922

Old Til

Olgan am I, first-born and noblest son of Til,
Emperor of far dominion sea to sea.
Olgan am I, praying that I may be
Father as kingly as mine own to me.
Olgan of the Blind Eyes, given by the gods
So that my vision might be kingly, and my will.

Othan am I, second and fairest son of Til,
Othan the Limbless, and so born to be,
For the all-seeing gods, then fearing me
Lest I should injure Olgan, that could see,
Gave me no limbs to injure; yea, ye gods,
I reck not, yet pray for my sire — he sorrows still.

Borsad am I, youngest and saddest son of Til,
Sad and made desolate beyond my years.
Borsad the Dumb, Borsad of the Maimed Ears,
Fit but for woman's sorrowing and tears.
Who made me thus? Ah, I could tell, but dumb
Is tongue and heart and soul of me; all still.

Old Til am I, emperor from sea to sea,
Brother of that great king whom men called Til,
Which is my secret and my secret still.
For I was like to him, and he to me
That none knew us apart save only one,
His eldest Olgan, Olgan of the Blind Eyes,
Blind that he might not know the foul deed done.
But Til swore dying that his second son
Would venge him, but I tore him limb from limb,
Othan the Limbless, I am safe from him.

But when the infant Borsad waxed and grew
There waxed and grew some knowledge in his eyes,
Some inborn knowledge, some god-sent surmise,
So frighted me, that I whom men call wise,
Made Borsad dumb, Borsad of the Maimed Ears.

They thinking these god-given, thank the gods
And spend in praying all their empty years,
While Old Til rules their empire sea to sea.

Pietermaritzburg, 22 September 1923
Natal University College Magazine, 1923

Felip

What, señor? — not want to go back? — if you knew!
If you knew but the half that I know, would you doubt?
But 'tis dull stuff to tell — what, you will have it out?
Listen then, señor — I will tell it to you.

Well, señor, the place — Dios, it was old —
Lay by the sierra — half-dead — half-asleep,
Sometimes half-scared of its wits by Felip',
My blood-friend, señor — from birth, I was told.

Felip', madre dios! — a name that they feared —
The devil's own spawn! — and many a name
Of the like — señor, I tell to their shame
They watched that Felip' was not near when they sneered.

Felip'! — scum of Hell! — and the Devil's Own! —
Sí, he smiled when he heard them, once in a while —
Even the padre said that his smile
Would have melted the heart of God on His throne.

How we loved him, señor — what purpose to weep?
Could caballero so handsome live like a monk?
I remember — he came to vespers — dead drunk —
And the padre prayed all night for Felip'.

Friends, I and Felip' — we swore by the name
Of some saint that we knew — some old fellow with hair
All over his face like a goat, but there
It has gone — what, señor? — sí, that is the same.

The village — they loved us for all of our sin —
The old village — Dios! it was old,
Old houses — old people — more fit for the mould
Of the churchyard than for life and its din.

Then the war — Felip' heard the news at the mill,
We were both on the road when an hour had passed,

41

Back we looked on the village — that look was our last —
Dios! — would you believe they were blubbering still.

We fought in the war, did I and Felip' —
Rebels in daytime or just when you please,
At night with the bugs and the rats and the fleas,
Felip' said he swore that bugs never sleep.

Ah señor! — Felip' — Dios! what a man!
I sickened of fever — they dropped me behind —
I crept to a hut half-dead and half-blind,
And swore all the oaths that an honest man can.

And Felip'! — he deserted after a mile
For was he not sworn to me by the blood?
Dios! what a man — all covered with mud,
Yet smiling señor! — I told you — that smile?

One day he left me alone in the hut,
A brave deed, señor! there were rebels about.
I can half remember his creeping out
To get me some blankets and water and fruit.

And I waited — well, yes — an hour or two,
Till I heard the sudden sound of a shot
And the sound of a gallop swift from the trot,
And I dragged myself to the door and looked through.

And I heard that laugh that I knew so well,
And I saw Felip' on the run through the wood,
His arms were heavy with blankets and food,
And — señor! — I cannot tell.

Señor! — Dios! what a man to weep!
Yet señor! — go back to the place?
His mother — she kissed me, she patted my face,
"Felip' over you, you over Felip'."

And he ran — sí, he ran — just a few yards more,
Nearer and nearer and nearer they rode,

And he smiled at me with the smile of a god.
And señor — I shut the door.

And he waited there for a while till they came,
Quite silent — I knew he was smiling at Death,
I heard the bayonets turn in his breath,
And I knew that he smiled just the same.

And I heard the hoof-beats die in the wood
Till all was silence as before,
And señor! — I dared not open the door
To Felip' — and his blankets — and food.

And I lay there señor, the devil's own while,
And tried to remember the padre's prayers,
But I could only remember a saint with hairs
And the dread of a dead man's smile.

And because I could not look on his face,
I tore a hole in the far-off wall,
So señor, you know now that you know all
Why I cannot go back to the place.

Natal University College Magazine, 1924

The Poet

Your prison in a word
Or in the song
Of some sweet bird
A magic that was dead
And doubts more anguishéd
Than our philosophies
Had ever heard.

You with some trick of phrase
At one leap scale the walls
And tread the heights of truth.
I hear your calls
As I swim moats, climb battlements;
I tell myself
You know not what you do
And all my life of days
Wish I had gone with you.

Pietermaritzburg, 6 May 1931
Unpublished

The Future

Night over farm, over furrow falling,
Stealing apace as the day gives room,
Brown priest, from the sanctuary calling
Litany of the magic gloom.

Brown priest from the hidden altar
Lost in a river of trees that weep,
Calling in tones that liquidly falter
Earth and the sons of earth to sleep.

Call from the shadow under the starkness
Mountains rimmed with the red of sun,
Celebrate the mass of the darkness,
Call to slumber, melodious one.

Brown priest of the gloom, go calling
Pain forgot in the dark's respite,
Chant of the silver plummets falling,
Silver stones in the well of night.

Natal University College Magazine, 1933

45

The Bull-frog

Upon the vlei the bull-frog croaks
    For beauty of the moon,
His song to ears of human folks
    Is slightly out of tune.

Can in his cold repulsive breast
    Stir passion or desire?
What knows his dank and humid chest
    Of the poetic fire?

What seeks his moist and beady gaze
    The far-off stars among?
What dreams has he of distant days
    When he was free and young?

Silence, old fool; and spare the moon
    Your harsh discordant croak.
The snobbish stars regard your tune
    As somewhat of a joke.

He dived beneath the moonlit ooze
    To hide his broken heart,
Like men when publishers refuse
    Their latest works of art.

Natal University College Magazine, 1933

Translation

From the Hindustani

Life was bitter, be that said,
So I prayed my God for a small knife.
For thus I reasoned, if I be dead,
What matter how bitter be life?

God was bitter, be that said,
For He sent me never a small knife.
He sent me a woman, a woman instead,
So what matter how bitter be life?

The woman was bitter, be that said,
So I prayed my God for a small knife.
For thus I reasoned, if she be dead,
What matter how bitter be life?

God was bitter, be that said,
For He sent me a knife, a small knife.
And now I'll hang till I be dead,
So what matter how bitter be life?

Park Rynie, 25 September 1934
Natal University College Magazine, 1934

Lied van die Verworpenes

,Kyk ma, daar kom die ossewaens,
Hoe trots waai daar die mooi vlae!'
,Gaan uit my kind en groet'nis sê
Vir helde van die vroeëre dae.'

Hy hardloop uit, my skat, my kind,
Ek hoor sy stem ,hip hip hoera!'
Dierbare God, hy loop reg voor
Die osse van die ossewa.

Rustig die edel jukgediert
Stap aan, sy arme lyfie oor.
Onkeerb're wiele kraak en dreun
Dis al wat nou die skare hoor.

O drome van die toekoms skoon
Wat ek vir jou my kleintjie had,
O Pad van ons Suid-Afrika,
Was dit nie ook my kind se pad?

19 December, 1938
Contact, 1957

Literal translation:

Song of the Outcasts:
'Look ma, here come the ox-wagons,/ How proudly the beautiful flags
wave!'/ 'Go out my child and greet/ The heroes of the earlier days.'//
He runs out, my treasure, my child,/ I hear his voice, 'Hip, Hip,
Hooray!'/ Dear God, he steps right in front/ of the oxen of the ox-
wagon.// Languidly the noble yoked beast/ Tramps on his weak body./
Unstoppable wheels creak and groan/ That is all that the crowds now
hear.// O dreams of the bright future/ That I had for you my little
child,/ O Road of our South Africa,/ Was it not my child's road too?

48

SONGS OF DISCOVERY AND AFFIRMATION

Reverie

1
The lonely road winds on, and is lost in the mist and the dark;
The hills loom wet and grotesque in the place of the dead,
Where seldom a man has trod and never a man has dwelt.
Silence unearthly there reigns, not a cry or a bark
Or a step, or even a bird that passes o'erhead
With a whirr of wings, and leaves me alone on the veldt.

2
As the road goes ever before, and I draw nearer the end,
And men that are younger than I take my place in the world;
As I draw near the last of life's leavings, the last of life's breath,
As steps that were confident falter, and proud shoulders bend,
Let me die with my purpose unaltered, my banner unfurled,
And I know! — I shall not be alone, ev'n in Death.

3
When sound of battle draws near, and I balance the wrong and the right
And the call of a world of wrong confuses my ears,
And I tremble and know that who stands for the right stands alone,
Then give me blood of a man, and forgive me my fears,
Let me stand in Death's face till he claim me his own,
And I feel I shall not be alone, in the fight.

Paton to Pearse, 10 June 1923
Unpublished

House of Dreams

. . . this old grey homestead by the road,
That stands in sweet seclusion, half stately and half sad,
Save when the roar of lions in some far-off kloof
Disturbs the solemn silence of the still abode.
Its quiet avenues unmarked by wheel or hoof,
But yellowed under by the leaves, that too have clad
The still green lawns against the cold.

The creepers, in a blaze of purple, red and gold,
Trailing untended, run mad riot round the roof;
And in and out the lattices and shady bowers,
Strewing the ground beneath with wanton artistry,
The yellow honeysuckles wind, and Golden Showers,
That let their long lobes fall with every breeze.
Then garlanding the paths are flaming beds of flowers,
That bend their graceful heads to hear in ecstasy
The sighing wind wash softly in the trees.

Signed K.S.
Natal University College Magazine, 1923

50

Song

The batteries are working and the great stamps roar,
And the great dumps are growing day by day,
And they mind me of the sand-dunes on the hot Hlabeni shore,
And the waving fields of sugar far away.

There are great green hills there and great winds blowing,
And white clouds sailing in the skies;
And a sound of quiet waters to their long rest flowing
Down the green valleys where the great sea lies.

There's a hot sun burning on long hot sands
And hot winds rustling in the cane,
Oxen ploughing on the long hot lands
When I get home again.

When I flee from the stamps to the quiet hills' keeping,
Flee the batteries' clamour to my little white place,
I can see my fields in the green valley sleeping.
And the roses round the doorway and my old woman's face.

Natal University College Magazine, 1925

Tugela, Tugela, sweep on . . .

Tugela, Tugela, sweep on, sweep on.
Thro' mountain and fastness
And bare krantz and wildness,
Sweep on.
In unwearying patience,
Inscrutable silence,
Thy myriad aloes
Stand dead with thy secret,
Sweep on, sweep on.

Mother of Rivers,
Daughter of Wildness,
Flow on
With wild sun-hot beauty
Thy desolate thorns
And thy myriad aloes
Keep thy mystery yet,
Flow on.

Thy towering peaks
Stand alone and aloof
Over thee.
Thy mystery sleeps
In invincible heights,
In the cave and the kloof
Where the aasvogels go.
Bury deep what they know
In the sea.

Paton to Pearse, 9 January 1925
Unpublished and untitled

52

Carton

As if unknowing of the sullen roar,
That surges round him like an angry sea,
As if uncaring what his death may be
Or what they clamour, clamour, clamour for,
He heeds not their bloodthirsty tumult or
The tumbrils rumbling past him ceaselessly,
But guards her weakness very tenderly,
And whispers 'Sister, but a little more.'
Then kisses her and sends her to her place,
And sadly watches the fast-falling knife
Till on his dissolute and wasted face
Shines radiant glory, and tranquillity,
'I am the Resurrection and the Life,'
One last hoarse murmur — silence — twenty-three.

Trouble not, son; I do not fear to die,
Not that my weak soul has no room for fear
God knows that my few days on his earth here
Were not heroic days, but days that I,
Had I the power to do the thing, would try
To polish over, now that death is near.
'Tis scarce to be called courage, yet 'tis queer
I have no fear of death, now death is by.
For I have seen the kindnesses of death
Frail pain worn souls borne by his gentle hand
Into the valleys of eternal rest;
The agony that strives for each last breath
Is Life's, not death's — it is his form that stands
In patient silence waiting — he knows best.

Paton to Pearse 9 January 1925
Unpublished

53

Sonnet

There's no way carved yet, no applauding crowd
To watch my lonely figure in the mist,
Scaling the peaks I longed for. No clenched fist
Has struck the table of the world and cowed
Rapacious men. But head's a little bowed
And mind from dreams a little does desist,
And soul in prayer a little does persist,
And voice in argument's but half as loud.
Yet free my mind from dreams and soul from prayer
And I'd be rather dead than so alive
To find within myself so little there.
I'll yield the peaks if it be mine to strive
To reach some gentle summit amply trod
And stand more humbly in the sight of God.

Park Rynie, 25 September 1934
Natal University College Magazine, 1934

From where the sun pours . . .

From where the sun pours on the southern sand
From break of day to the declining hour
His fierce and unabating southern power
I come, to this austere and northern land.
The child of sun is driven by the rain
Along the streets, to welcome with a cry
The first thin breaking of the northern sky,
That breaks, that closes, till it rains again!
Yet these are things outside us. Talk of friends
For Nature's cruelty makes high amends.
The sun is in the mind, the heart, the mouth,
And in the rooms where friends are met together,
It shines, regardless of the northern weather,
With all the power of the golden South.

Paton to Dorrie Paton, 15 September 1946
Unpublished and untitled

54

Singer of Childhood

Singer of childhood, do you remember
How the child struggled to capture your song?
Or was it your forerunner sang to the one
Who was the forerunner of this one now singing?

How the child struggled to write down your song
To capture your notes that went dropping and dropping
Deeper and deeper into the caverns of melody.
Yet it was not your notes that he wanted,
But something behind them, beyond them, within them.
Some sorrow, some agony, some unfathomable meaning,
And he wrote it all down in hiding and privacy
And feverishly searching the secret transcriptions
Could find not one line, not one sentence or syllable
Not one infinitesimal fragment
Of your music, eluding him.

Do you yourself know the contents
Of your songs? Did your forerunner
Know the contents of the songs he intoned
To the forerunner of this one now singing?

Singer of childhood, there shall never be captured now
The song that your forerunner sang to the child.
For age has corrupted it, the deep notes sound deeper
The sorrowful more sorrowful, the deepest concluding
Tell me no longer of the well-loved river
Of childhood, but intone to me Africa
The whole continent of rivers and streams
And its thousand sorrowful songs.

Sing me again, morning and evening
The songs of my childhood which your forerunner
Sang with no deeper intention
To the forerunner of this one now singing.

Maybe if you sing to me, morning and evening
Your songs which had no deeper intention
Maybe I shall capture the first flawless agony
The unspeakable meaning, the unspeakable sadness
And loveliness, the terror and tenderness,
Of man's home and the earth. Yet also perhaps
It is the foreknowledge, the secret intimation
Of age's corruption, of the fears and the hates
Of the world, that hushes the voices
Of barefooted boys, and makes them stand silent
In the undergrowth, listening with adoration
To your notes dropping and dropping
Deeper and deeper into caverns of melody.

Anerley, 21 November 1948
Unpublished

In the Umtwalumi Valley

In the deep valley of the Umtwalumi
In its tribal valley with its kaffirboom
Red, red, and red again along the banks
We in our swiftly moving car
Pass small boys on the road walking
And they call out in their own language
For pleasure or hope of gain, I cannot say,
Their salutations, father, father.

Yes, I will not forget your salutations
I sit here pondering the deep meanings
The solemn and sacred meanings
Of your salutations
I sit here pondering the obligations
The solemn and sacred obligations
Of your words shouted in passing.

Anerley, 1949
Knocking on the Door, 1975

56

The mist comes down . . .

The mist comes down from height and hill
And hides the farms below,
And clothes in silence and in peace
A distant land I know.

The farmhouse fire crackles warm
Within the farmhouse walls
And in the wet and lonely dark
The titihoya calls.

The ghostly trees loom up at me
And drop their ghostly rain
And all the world is ghostly still
Beyond the window pane.

The days are gone to lie me down
In bracken wet and cold.
To twine the grass and kiss the earth
The days have made me old.

So when I wish to go again
In scenes of ghostly joy
I stand behind the window pane
And send the ghostly boy.

And there will he lie down for me
The eager ghostly boy
And he will kiss the sodden earth
With strange and eager joy.

And he will feel him in his heart
The strange and stabbing twist
That comes to some that answer there
To a lone bird in mist.

Yet if I could be there but now
I'd leap the years again
And stand me in the ghostly trees
And taste how salt the rain.

Lane's Flat, 3 January 1950
Unpublished and untitled

I came to a valley . . .

I

1. I came to a valley where it was winter, and sat myself down on a rock. The whole world was quiet, and the hills lay as if sleeping.

2. The farms spread out below me, where the reaping was finished. I saw the great heaps of the unshelled cobs, like white hillocks under the sun.

3. The stalks of maize stood in the fields, and the cattle moved amongst them. They snapped off the stalks as they moved, and these distant sounds came faintly up to me.

4. The whole world was drenched in the peace of the sun, and the smoke from some house went slowly upwards. The rock was warm at my back, and I joined the valley in sleeping.

5. And the voice of my Lord came to me, saying take up thy pen and write. But I was deep in slumber, and made no answer to him.

6. And the voice of my Lord came again to me, saying take up thy pen and write. And I answered saying to him, I have no things for writing.

7. And the voice said, look at thy side. And I looked and there were pen and paper. So I answered him saying, what shall I write?

8. And the voice said, this and this shalt thou write. But I said to the Lord, where then is my peace?

9. For how shall man utter such words? And who is there that shall read them? For the tongue that speaks them shall be burned with fire, and the eyes that read them be stricken with blindness.

10. And the angry shall rise up against me, with wrath for their children's sake. And my own shall be fatherless, and go homeless upon the earth.

11. And the voice said, shall I wait then for thy son, or tarry for thy son's son? Shall the whole world be patient, because thou art afraid?

12. Therefore I took the pen and the paper, and could hardly write for my trembling. But my heart trembled also, therefore these words are but faintly the words of my Lord.

II

1. I slept and saw a vision of a certain man that took a wild beast that he feared, and fenced it in with wood and iron. He fenced it in both high and strong, and gave all his mind to his labour.

2. And the beast moved to and fro in the place of its captivity, and filled day and night with its roaring. It ceased not from roaring, nor from moving to and fro in its captivity.

3. But the fence was stout and strong, and the wood and iron built for enduring. And the man laughed at the roaring of the beast, and he slept, and his fear slept with him.

4. And sometimes the beast was sullen, and moved to and fro unceasingly. And sometimes it was full of fury, and broke its teeth on the wood and iron, and threw itself against the fence in rage and anger.

5. And the man's friends said to him, make the fence yet stronger. Or build another round the first, against the day of disaster.

6. So he built a second round the first, stouter and stronger. And the beast was moved to yet greater anger, and threw itself against the barricades with fury and roaring.

7. And it broke down the first, and dashed itself against the second, which was stouter and stronger. And the man's fear returned to him, and he builded himself a third, even stouter and stronger.

8. He builded it from early to late, because of the fear within him. And his house lacked for food, and his children were hungry, because of the fields that lay fallow, and the oxen that stood idle.

9. And when they complained to him, he was angered, that they saw not that he laboured for his children. And he said to them, wait till this fence is finished, then we shall eat and drink and be merry, because of the fear that is gone out of us.

10. And the beast broke through the second fence, but the third was stouter and stronger. Nevertheless for the sake of their peace, he built a fourth that was to be yet stouter and stronger.

11. And now he slept not, but laboured incessantly. Yet when he slept, he woke in fear, and went to his fence. And the beast went to and fro, and he to and fro with it; when the beast turned, he turned with it; when the beast slept, he slept with it; and when the beast rose from his sleep, the man rose also, and followed the beast.

12. And the beast broke through the third fence, and the man set himself to build a fifth. He scoured the land for wood and iron, and impoverished himself. He heard not the song of the birds, and the rain was no benefaction to him. For his thought was the thought of the beast, and he had no thought for the pleasure and labour of a man.

13. And in my dream I cried out to him, man, thou art in captivity. And taken unawares he woke from his sleep, and stretched out his arms to me, and I saw the anguish of his eyes. And he would have answered me, but that the beast was awakened by my cry, and roared with anger and fury, and went to and fro in its captivity. And the man rose and followed him, and had no more ears and eyes for me, and I watched him with pity, till I too awoke, and saw neither man nor beast in the valley.

III

1. The voice of the Lord came unto me saying, go thou into the valley that is called Beautiful, unto the house of the King that is called Conqueror, and knock on the door of his house, and speak the words that are given unto thee.

2. And I answered the Lord, how shall I go to this king? For thou knowest that I am a stranger, and how shall I speak to him who possesses me?

3. And the Lord said, shall I wait for thy son, and for the son of thy son? Therefore I prepared myself for my journey, because of the anger of the Lord.

4. And I went over the plain that is called Outstretched, where the grass was tall and red and yellow; and the great hills lay sleeping and silent, and the sun of the winter was over the whole earth.

5. And after many days I came to the valley that is called Beautiful, where is the forest of tall trees and shadows; and with

61

fear and trembling I came to the house of the king, and knocked on the door of his house.

6. Yet they did not open to me, they spoke to me through a small window. And the house was barred and bolted, and the walls of it were sheathed in iron and brass.

7. And the King said, who art thou that comest to the forest of tall trees and shadows? Does thou not know that it is full of enemies, that will fall upon thee from every side?

8. And I answered, Oh King, I have seen no enemies, nor have I found a cause of fear, save the fear that is always in myself. And they said one to another, he speaketh the language of a stranger, and one that hath no understanding.

9. And the king said with anger, what seekest thou? And I said I bring a message from the Lord, even the King of Heaven.

10. And the king said, speak thy message. For no stranger shall enter this house.

11. Then said I, the King of Heaven speaketh unto the King of this land, even to the Conqueror. And he chargeth thee to put down the shutters and the bars, and to cast out the fear that is thine enemy.

12. Else said the Lord, thy fear shall eat thee up. For I have heard of thy laws and commandments, which thou hast made.

13. But I the Lord have laws and commandments. And thine abide for a generation, but mine abide for ever.

14. And thine are the fruits of fear, and shall renew themselves from day to day. But mine are the fruits of Love, and have no need of successors, being themselves eternal.

15. Come out Oh King that is called the Conqueror, and do battle with the things that thou fearest. For thy greatest enemy is in thine house, and will surely bring thee and thy people to destruction.

62

16. And the King said, who art thou a stranger to torment me? And who art thou to disturb my peace? Make haste and begone, lest I put the dogs at thee, and they tear the flesh from thy bones.

17. And I answered, myself trembling, Oh King, think not that peace can be captured. Nor canst thou hold it in with bolts and bars, nor make it captive with thy commandments.

18. Therefore I left the country that is called Beautiful, and returned to my place. And the Lord said, have hope of him, for that he said that thou tormentedst him.

IV

1. And I slept and saw a vision, of a man and a child walking, hand in hand. And so walking, they went through the world.

2. And the child was gay and laughing, and was full of pleasure; but the man was dark and silent, and his eyes were vigilant and afraid.

3. And the child stretched out his hand for a flower, but the man restrained him saying, the flower is beautiful, but the seeds may be the seeds of death.

4. And the child stretched out his hand for a fawn, but the man restrained him saying, it is playful and tender, but no man knows the day when it may kill with its horns.

5. And the child saw a flashing stream with water, murmuring through bracken and ferns, but the man restrained him saying, there is water enough at home.

6. So they passed through the world, teaching and learning; and the man clutched tighter the hand of the child, and the child the hand of the man.

7. And they came to an open place where nothing was, save the great yellow plains under the sun; and the man stopped and trembled, and said, here is the greatest danger of all.

8. And I saw the child going forward, but I knew that it saw nothing; and it turned and looked at the man with perplexity.

9. And it saw the agony and fear of the man, and it stopped and trembled also. And together they fled from the dangerous place.

Undated: probably written in the early 1950s
Unpublished and untitled

I Have Approached

I have approached a moment of sterility
I shall not write any more awhile
For there is nothing more meretricious
Than to play with words.
Yet they are all there within me
The great living host of them
The gentle, the compassionate
The bitter and the scornful
The solemn and the sorrowful
The words of the childhood that will not come again.
But they do not come out for nothing
They do not form themselves into meanings
Unless some price has been paid for them
Unless some deep thing is felt that runs
Like a living flame through their shapes and forms
So that they catch fire and fuse themselves
Into glowing incandescences
Or if the felt thing is deep indeed,
Into conflagrations, so that the pen
Smokes in the hand, and the hand
Burns to the bone, and the paper chars
Under the heat of composition.
Therefore words, stay where you are awhile
Till I am able to call you out,
Till I am able to call you with authentic voice
So that the great living host of you
Tumble out and form immediately
Into parties, commandos, and battalions
Briefly saluting and wheeling away instantly
To waken the sleeping consciences
To call back to duty the absenting obligations
To assault again, night and day, month and year
The fortresses and bastions of our fears.

Undated: probably written between 1948 and 1949
Contrast, 1961

To Walt Whitman

Barefooted boy on Paumanok's shore,
I, not a boy any longer,
I, having waited longer than you,
Being a man now, dare not wait any longer,
For in me too there are a thousand songs,
And some more sorrowful than yours.

And why did he not sing before? Why, duties,
Duties and resolutions, programmes and crusades,
Solemn undertakings, religious obligations,
And plans to revolutionise the world,
All crowded in upon him, till night came,
And pen stared at paper, waiting for a voice
That never spoke. So head fell on arms
And pen on paper, and the singer slept
With no song sung, waking again with day
To duties and resolutions, programmes, and crusades,
And solemn undertakings. Yes, and woke afraid
That the great living host of tumbling words
Was a delusion, a brood of children
Locked within a womb that ne'er would open.
He pressed his ears to the dividing wall
Hearing the crying to be born, and knew
With joy them yet alive, and knew with fear
Them yet unborn. And all the while a voice
Mocked him for barrenness, a mocker struck
The full-bellied womb with careless hands
Striking the frail, the tender things,
Saying, bring them forth, the singing children,
The gay and lovely ones, the sorrowful,
Mocking and saying, bring them forth,
Singer without a song.

And once when he awoke so, deep afraid
Hearing the voice, the voice, the mocking voice,
Saying, bring them forth, the singing children,
The gay and lovely ones, the sorrowful,

Bring them forth, singer without a song,
He stopped his ears, shrinking from this tormenting,
But this voice possessed him, entered his body
By what way he knew not, filling the heart,
The mind, the soul, calling from within him,
Louder than any voice he ever knew,
Until he heard, he who had waited endlessly,
Until he heard, astonished, scarcely believing,
It was commanding, not mocking any longer,
Commanding, bring them forth, the singing children,
The gay and lovely ones, the sorrowful.
And when he would have spoken, it spoke before him,
Saying all he thought of saying, duties,
Resolutions, plans, programmes and crusades,
All these a time are ended, go and sing.
And he, astonished, scarcely believing, cried
What shall I sing? And this voice said, sing
What else but Africa, songs of Africa,
The thousand sorrowful songs?

So now, great brother, I am ready to sing now.
These songs shall be presented to you
And what does it matter if they are unworthy,
If they are not so gay and sorrowful as I thought,
For I have a feeling to give them to you,
I, not really a stranger, have a desire to speak to you
And why not speak to you with these?

Anerley, 8 August 1948
Knocking on the Door, 1975

68

THIRD JOURNEY

POEMS OF CONSCIENCE

POLITICS AND PHILANTHROPY

I Take This Africa

I take this Africa this continent
Unto myself, nothing rejecting,
    No man no beast no danger
And I am penitent.

Undated but probably written in 1950
Unpublished

(See Notes at the end for further references to the various poems)

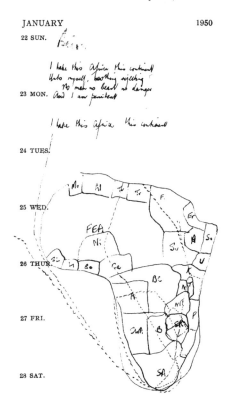

70

We Mean Nothing Evil Towards You

Black man, we are going to shut you off
We are going to set you apart, now and forever.
We mean nothing evil towards you
You shall have your own place, your own institutions.
Your tribal customs shall flourish unhindered
You shall lie all day long in the sun if you wish it
All the things that civilisation has stolen
Shall be restored. You shall take wives
Unhindered by our alien prohibitions
Fat-bellied children shall play innocently
Under the wide-branching trees of the lush country
Where you yourselves were born.
Boys shall go playing in the reed lagoons
Of far Ingwavuma, the old names
Shall recover old magic, milk and honey
Shall flow in the long-forsaken places
We mean nothing evil towards you.

A fresh new wind shall blow through your territory
Under your hands freed from our commandment
You shall build what shall astonish you.
The ravished land shall take on virginity
The rocks and the shales of the desolate country
Shall acquire the fertility of the fruitful earth.
Chance-gotten children shall return to the womb
To re-emerge with sanctions and live pattern lives
Of due obedience to authority and age.
Morality shall be recovered, the grave
And fearless bearing, the strange innocence
Of the tribal eyes, and all the sorrows
Of these hundred years shall pass away
This is our reparation, our repayment
Of the incomputable debt.
We mean nothing evil towards you.

Can you for whom we have made this reparation
Not give us something also, not petition
The gods of all the tribes we recreate
To call you back in one migration
North to the beating heart of Africa?
Can you not make a magic that will silence conscience,
Put peace behind the frowning vigilant eyes,
That will regardless of Space and Time
Wipe you from the face of the earth?
But without pain . . .
For we mean nothing evil towards you.

Our resolve is immutable, our hands tremble
Only with the greatness of our resolution.
We are going to set you apart, now and forever,
We mean nothing evil towards you.

Anerley, 11 August 1948
Knocking on the Door, 1975

Could You Not Write Otherwise?

Could you not write otherwise, this woman said to me,
Could you not write of things really poetical?
Of many-coloured birds dipping their beaks
Into many-coloured flowers?
Of mine machinery standing up, you know,
Gaunt, full of meaning, against the sky?

Must you write always of black men and Indians,
Of half-castes and Jews, Englishmen and Afrikaners,
Of problems insoluble and secret fears
That are best forgotten?
You read the paper, you post your letters,
You buy at the store like any normal being.
Why then must you write such things?

Madam, really, since you ask the question,
Really, Madam, I do not like to mention it
But there is a voice that I cannot silence.
It seems I have lived for this, to obey it
To pour out the life-long accumulation
Of a thousand sorrowful songs.
I did not ask for this destination
I did not ask to write these same particular songs.

Simple I was, I wished to write but words,
And melodies that had no meanings but their music
And songs that had no meaning but their song.
But the deep notes and the undertones
Kept sounding themselves, kept insistently
Intruding themselves, like a prisoned tide
That under the shining and the sunlit sea
In caverns and corridors goes underground thundering.

Madam, I have no wish to be cut off from you
I have no wish to hurt you with the meanings
Of the land where you were born
It was with unbelieving ears I heard

My artless songs become the groans and cries of men.
And you, why you may pity me also,
For what do I do when such a voice is speaking,
What can I speak but what it wishes spoken?

Anerley, 17 August 1948
Knocking on the Door, 1975

The Laughing Girls

I hear the noise of the loud laughing girls
Laughing around the house, distracting me
And should I go to them and say
Go away and leave me some silence
For I am writing the sorrowful meanings
Of your race, why they would laugh at me
And say in their own tongue to one another
This man is mad. They would laugh more loudly
Derisively, not apprehending
The sorrowful meaning of themselves.

But should I go to them and say
Go away and leave me some silence
Or I shall telephone to the police,
Why they would leave me then
Still laughing perhaps, but less loudly,
Half bravely and half afraid,
Their laughter dying away down the street,
Saying in their own tongue to one another,
Yes let us move away. They would laugh half bravely,
Half afraid, yet dimly apprehending
The sorrowful meaning of themselves.

Anerley, 17 August 1948
Knocking on the Door, 1975

74

The Discardment

We gave her a discardment
A trifle, a thing no longer to be worn,
Its purpose served, its life done.
She put it on with exclamations
Her eyes shone, she called and cried,
The great bulk of her pirouetted
She danced and mimed, sang snatches of a song.
She called out blessings in her native tongue
Called to her fellow servants
To strangers and to passers-by
To all the continent of Africa
To see this wonder, to participate
In this intolerable joy.

And so for nothing
Is purchased loyalty and trust
And the unquestioning obedience
Of the earth's most rare simplicity
So for nothing
The destruction of a world.

Anerley, 8 October 1948
Knocking on the Door, 1975

75

Dancing Boy

Small boy I remember you
I remember you used to dance here
By the roadside
And the white people stopped in their cars
And when you had finished dancing
Gave money to you.

Sir, I am the one indeed
I remember you stopped in your car
And when I had finished dancing
Gave money to me.

Small boy you are the one indeed
But why are you not dancing?
Do you not dance here any more?

Sir, I do not dance here any more
For one day when I was dancing
A white man stopped here in his car
And he came at me trembling
Like nothing I had seen before
And he thrust money at me
Great piles of paper money
Into my very hands and cried
For God's sake and for Christ's sake
Do not dance here any more.

I took this money to my father
And he said to me
It's a deep thing and a dark thing
And I do not understand it
But you must not dance there any more.
Sir, that is why
Although I am the one indeed
I do not dance here any more.

Johannesburg, 4 November 1948
Knocking on the Door, 1975

76

Indian Woman

You, Indian woman in the rain,
Do you not see me coming?
Do you not see it is a white person coming
In his automobile?
What, you will not yield?
Neither will I then
And the brown-coloured mud
Rises in a fountain bespattering
Your stubborn garments.

My God, but your hair is white as snow
I did not know you were so old, Indian woman
For had I known you were so old
I would have conceded something
I would have bespattered you
Not quite so venomously.

Anerley, 10 November 1948
Knocking on the Door, 1975

The Stock Exchange

And he said — it was two in the morning then —
Let us hurry home, sleep, rise, bath, and dress
And meet on the floor of the Stock Exchange
And there you and I shall stand up and cry out
Against injustices.

And I said, I can hardly wait for daylight,
I can hardly wait to stand up and cry out
Against injustices.

So we went to the floor of the Stock Exchange
And I failed to see him though I looked everywhere
And he failed to see me though he looked everywhere
And we failed therefore to stand up and cry out
Against injustices.

But we are meeting again some time soon
To work out some better, even more vivid plan
Whereby we shall stand up and cry out
Against injustices.

Anerley, 20 November 1948
Knocking on the Door, 1975

Durban

The voice of God over Durban crying
Over the white men and the Indians
Over the merchants and the politicians
Of the proud city.

The voice of Christ over Durban crying
No, not the meek and the mild Jesus,
But he who drove from the temple
The money-changers.

Come down O Lord of Man and Heaven
To a round table of white men and Indians
That when you have finished instructing us
We may crucify you.

Undated, but probably Anerley, 1948
Knocking on the Door, 1975

78

To a Person Who Fled to Rhodesia

I remember that you told me that you loved South Africa
The sun, the orange trees red with their fruit
And the kaffirboom red with its flowers
And the great spaces in gold apparel.
But you were afraid of the beasts of the veld
That growled about the barricades in the dark
And tormented your dreams.
I remember I told you their name
Quaestio Africana

And you said to me, I am frightened here,
I am going to Rhodesia.

I remember I visited you in Rhodesia
And how you were overjoyed to find
That the sun shone the same
That the orange trees red with their fruit
And the kaffirboom red with its flowers
And the great spaces in gold apparel
Were the same.
And you showed me with pride
And a certain knowing reproach
The pet that you kept in your house,
So small and gambolling,
And how you were angry with me
When I said to you, Rhodesian,
Look north if you fear to look south
Look east or look west but look sharp
For this is none else but the young
Quaestio Africana.

Dated 1948
Contact, 1958

79

2 SUN.

3 MON.

4 TUES.

5 WED.

6 THUR.

7 FRI.

8 SAT.

NY 4/4/49

I ask you, Indian people . . .

I ask you, Indian people, where do you turn to now?
Where shall you find now safety and peace?
Where shall you hide now, Indian Woman,
And you, little child, what can your father do now?

What help have I for you now?
I have no guns and no ammunition,
What help have any for you now?
What voice is raised to speak to you?

My voice shall be raised to speak for you
I have no weapons but my words
But they are heard in many countries
I give you them now for your help.

I shall give you the best that I have
I shall make them sound like any noise of guns
I shall.

Anerley, 2 January 1949
Unpublished and untitled

Anxiety Song of an Englishman

Down here where we talked of the Empire
From morning till night, and heard not a word
Of Afrikaans spoken, now come the great engines
And the Afrikaners stand on the footplates
And look confidently down through the hissing steam
As though they themselves had manufactured them
Yes they look down confidently at me
From a great height it seems, and turn a lever
And move off majestically and contemptuously
To the next station, to dwarf some other person.

January, 1949
Knocking on the Door, 1975

To a Black Man Who Lost a Child Thro' Starvation

Black man standing weeping before me
I take your hand in my hands
I try to transmit unspoken to you
The sorrow of all white people.
Of bishops and predicants and apostolic evangelists
Of great magnates and millionaires and all masters
Of owners of factories and stockbrokers and their clerks
Of shop-girls and waitresses and lift-attendants
Of judges and magistrates and great lawyers
Of prosecutors and policemen and drivers of pick-up vans
I try to transmit their sorrow to you.

Black man standing weeping before me
I try to transmit unspoken to you
The compassion of all white people
Of Englishmen and Afrikaners and Jews
Of Governors-General and Prime Ministers and Administrators
Of Senators and Members of Parliament
Of the people of Parktown and Musgrave Road and
        Rondebosch
And Vrededorp and Greyville and Salt River
Of Communists and Nationalists and the United Party
I try to transmit their compassion to you.

Black man, standing weeping before me
I transmit unspoken, words of atonement
And reparation. I try to transmit to you
The atonement and reparation of the rich.
Of the eaters of asparagus and stuffed olives
Of the drinkers of champagne and delicate wines
Of the frequenters of the Carlton and the Grand National
Of the Mount Nelson and the Royal and the Hilton
Of the Rand Club and all the Country Clubs
Of the Metro, the Playhouse, and the Alhambra
Of the generous givers of cocktail parties
Of the owners of incredible mansions
I try to transmit their atonement to you.

82

Black man standing weeping before me
I hide from you the words of my guilt
Of the guilt of all white persons
Of the idle and careless and thoughtless
Of the champions of self-preservation
Of the defenders of civilisation
Of the preachers of brotherly love.
Who else but the King of the Cross
Could have taken their sins upon Him?
Who else can make atonement and reparation
And transmit to you words of compassion?
Who else but the King of the Cross
Dare speak spoken words of your loss?

Paton to Mary Benson, 31 May 1949
Unpublished

~~(18)~~

VI Black Woman Teacher

Black woman teacher in distant Pondoland
Nameless woman teacher working your life out
Far from the lights & the sound & the cities
I said to you, your work is noted,
Your humble work is noted & remembered
It is known there in Johannesburg.

~~I never guessed to unlock such tumult~~
~~Such profound acceptance of the bonds~~
Of ~~acquiescence,~~

~~I never bargained to unlock such tumult~~
~~To loosen bonds of such profound acceptance~~
~~To wake such pride, believing, unbelieving,~~
~~To waken such long hidden hunger, such a pride~~
~~That suddenly unhooded like a queen~~
~~And stood before me swift & fierce & humble~~
~~To know this work was noted & remembered~~
~~By all the might & power of the land.~~
~~And like a fierce &~~
~~And swift & dark & fierce confronted me~~
~~Making me ashamed & humble.~~

I never guessed to unlock such tumult
To loosen such profound acceptance
Of the bonds of acquiescence, such pride
Hungry & fierce, believing, unbelieving,
That the humble work was noted & remembered
By the might & power & glory of the land.

To loosen such profound acquiescence
In ~~long~~ accepted bonds, such pride
Of hungry & swift & fierce & humble
That this work was noted & remembered
By the power & the majesty, the
{ might & the dominion
{ dominion & the glory

~~I never bargained to unlock such tumult~~
~~To loosen such profound acceptance of the bonds~~
~~Of acquiescence, to ~~unmask~~ wake such pride~~
~~Believing, unbelieving, fierce & hungry,~~
~~That the humble work was noted & remembered~~
~~By the might & power & glory of the land.~~

~~Hungry & swift & fierce & humble~~
~~That the nameless work was noted~~
~~& remembered~~
~~By the might & power & glory~~
~~of the land.~~

Black Woman Teacher

Black woman teacher in distant Bavendaland
Nameless woman teacher teaching your life out
Far from the lights and the sounds
 of the tumultuous cities
I said to you, your work is noted
Your humble work is noted and remembered
It is known there in Johannesburg.

I did not lie to you, your work is noted
Your humble work is noted and remembered
By some of us, here and there,
 in the tumultuous cities
Yet had it not been so I could have lied to you
To see the glad light in the eyes
The shy and earnest pride
That your humble work was noted and remembered
By the might and power and glory of the land.

Anerley, 14 September, 1949
Knocking on the Door, 1975

85

Samuel

The black boy rose from his bed
And came to me willingly
And master, master, he said,
Why did you call for me?

But I told him I called no word
And he said to me sheepishly
I must have dreamt that I heard
The master calling me.

And again he rose from his bed
And came to me willingly
And master, master, he said
Why did you call for me?

But I told him I called no word
And he said to me with shame
I dreamt again that I heard
The master calling my name.

And yet again from his bed
He came to me willingly
And master, master, he said
Why did you call for me?

Now God is great I know
But He can't quite understand
Or why should He summon so
Black boys in a white man's land?

I did not call, I said,
And I have no mind to call
For God's sake go to your bed
And answer no more at all.

London, 28 September 1949
Knocking on the Door, 1975

86

The Monument

The man stood by the monument
    And glorified his race
A hundred thousand clapped their hands
    Beneath that holy place.

Justice for all, I heard him say,
    Or let our race be cursed
In alphabetic order too
    By chance that puts us first.

And who shall say what justice is
    Or judge upon its fitness
And here he pointed up to heaven
    And said God be my witness.

From out the blue unclouded sky
    There came a bolt from heaven
And see it strikes the speaker down
    Right on the stroke of seven.

A hundred thousand on their knees
    And all perplexed and praying
For was it really impious
    All that this man was saying?

Lane's Flat, 16 December 1949
Unpublished

I'll stab the conscience . . .

I'll stab the conscience of the world awake
With fine-pointed barbs, and shafts of steel
Red-hot to follow, I'll uncover her,
Cut open her cold breast, and with brass gloves
Steel rasped and diamond-pointed get the frozen heart
To beating, and I'll hear her cries unmoved.

Lane's Flat, 19 December 1949
Unpublished and untitled

87

25/1/70

I am the stars over the trees, and the glory
I am not God, in fact I acknowledge them,
But I am the form of all that matter.
I sit on a table throne, but I came down from it
And say to the people, you fed me there,
And show your side, showed me.
They smile to look their ashes & take their power
And I smile down with them.

24/1/70

Hungry is the homeland
The cured [illegible]
Is uncontrollable fear
Yet keep silent till you be heard
The great winds freedom
Now about the homeland hills
that the stuff of one you are heard
This homeland is one toss

We speak now noble courage [illegible]
[illegible] thought [illegible] but naughty, great
[illegible] quickly say it so nightsheared

Unholy are the hungry feet
And homesteller on that I then
Where are die...
brother are my own brother
But they go. What my know like [illegible]
I ask, [illegible] what did you learn [illegible] ways?
the answer is my silence

Do not weep for me, ancestor
Weep for yourselves
For your day is gone.

You [illegible] me no longer
[illegible] for [illegible] go
See your child here
licked, coiled in sleep.
I do not weep to them
I do not ask this city [illegible]
My heart is [illegible] cold as stone.

But you live Zanzi [illegible] note
Some mother holds child?
They used thought for them like lords
the brothers off the homeland
Zanzi came, weary them
in [illegible] the constellation.
I cannot look at two eyes
that return, stay.
They have born to no [illegible]
While unbearable, the homeland hills,
The new freedom, the homeland death.
And the new winds singing death.

I am the trees and the trees and the glory
I came down from the throne
And say to the people, you fed me there
Here when you said, redeem me,
And they not trusty of me.
I stood on them, took [illegible] my smile
For I [illegible] you do not smile
Your [illegible] the homeland
Shall come ride lords to your house.

Alan Paton
26/1/70

I am the Law . . .

I am the Law, and the Power, and the Glory
I am not God, in fact I acknowledge Him.
I sit on a high throne, but I come down from it
And say to the people, you put me there,
And when you wish, remove me.
They smile and lick their chops, and taste their power
And I smile with them.

Hungry is the homeland
The crust of independence
Is unsatisfying bread
Yet keep silent lest you be heard
The great winds of freedom
Blow about the homeland hills
We speak our noble language
But quietly, lest it be heard.

Outside are the terrifying feet
And hammerblows on the door
Open or die.
These are my own brothers
Brothers of my homeland
But they go through my house like lords
I ask, where did you learn these things?
The answer is my blood.

Do not weep for me, ancestors
Weep for yourselves
For your day is gone.
See your child here
Silent, covered in blood.
I do not weep to them
I do not ask their pity
My heart is cold as stone.

Did you hear of Zuma's wife
Seven months with child?

They went through her house like lords
Her brothers of the homeland.
Zuma came hurrying home
In time for lamentation.
I cannot look at his eyes
They have seen a new thing
Quite unspeakable,
The new freedom of the homeland hills,
And the new winds bringing death.

I am the Law and the Power and the Glory
I come down from the throne
And say to the people, you put me there
And when you wish, remove me.
I shout at them, God damn you, smile
For if you do not smile
Your brothers of the homeland
Shall come like lords to your house.

Botha's Hill, February 1970
Unpublished and untitled

Death of a Priest

Most Honourable I knock at your door
I knock there by day and by night
My knuckles are raw with blood
I hope it does not offend you
To have these marks on your door.

I know you are there Most Honourable
I know that you hear my knocking
But you do not answer me
Pity my impotence I cannot reach your power
I cannot bring you my tale of sorrow
You may die and never know
What you have done or you may fall
And leave no chance of its undoing.

Most Honourable the sorrow is not my own
It is of a man who has no hands to knock
No voice to cry. A sorrow so deep
That if you had it for your own
You would cry out in unbelieving anguish
That such a thing could be.

Most Honourable do not bestir yourself
The man is dead
He fell down the stairs and died
And all his wounds can be explained
Except the holes in his hands and feet
And the long deep thrust in his side.

Botha's Hill, 14 March 1970
Knocking on the Door, 1975

[The Imam Haron, a Moslem leader who had been arrested under the Terrorism Act, died in prison
in mysterious circumstances in September 1969.]

Caprivi Lament

Makwela, Ikgopoleng, and you two Sibekos,
what were you fighting for?
Makwela, was it for your house in Springs
and your security of tenure?
Or did you fight for me and my possessions
and this big room where I write to you,
a room as big as many houses?

Sibeko of Standerton, what did you die for?
Was it for the schooling of your children?
Were you so hungry for their learning
or were you fighting for the rich grand schools
of my own children?

Sibeko of Bloemfontein, was it for those green pastures
of your own Free State country
that you poured out your young man's blood?
Was it for the sanctity of family life
and the infinitude of documents?
Or were you fighting to protect me
and my accustomed way of life?

Ikgopoleng of Lichtenburg,
was it South Africa you fought for?
Which of our nations did you die for?
Or did you die for my parliament
and its thousand immutable laws?
Did you forgive us all our trespasses
in that moment of dying?

I was not at your gravesides, brothers,
I was afraid to go there.
But I read the threnodial speeches
how you in life so unremembered
in death became immortal.

Away with your threnodial speeches, says the Lord.
Away with your solemn assemblies.
When you lift up your hands in prayer
I will hide my eyes from you.
Cease to do evil and learn to do right,
pursue justice and champion the oppressed.

I saw a new heaven and a new earth
for the first heaven and earth had passed away
and there was an end to death
and to mourning and crying and pain
for the old order had passed away.

Is that what you died for, my brothers?

Or is it true what they say
that you were led into ambush?

Botha's Hill, April 1973
Sunday Tribune, 1973

[In April 1973 a party of South African black policemen were ambushed in Caprivi Strip by guerrillas
operating from Zambia. Four of them were killed.]

1986

It is the children, my love, my love,
Oh this can I tell you, my love, my love.
It is our children, my husband, my love
It is our children who now enquire
That it is your wife who must wait your life
with the rudder I fear.

It will be tomorrow, my love, my love
It is tomorrow that they enquire
And I say that I cannot stay your
Then this commander may rest easy for me
the rudder I fear.

I send you a present, my love, my love,
Though not of my own desire
This commander and it's my duty, my love
This present I humbly beseech, my true
the rudder I fear.

They say I need not be forward, my love
To them at the forward shore
So long as you know that I shall be, my love
the rudder I fear.

It is the children, my love, my love
It is the children who now enquire
That I must wait you this present my love
the rudder I fear.

They say they must die for the cause, my love
But you say why the laws, my love
they say why they must die, my love
with the rudder I fear.

94

Necklace of Fire

They say I must send you a present, my love,
That is what the comrades require,
They say I must send you a necklace, my love,
A necklace of fire.
I told them I would not send it, my love,
A present so dire,
The children laughed in my face, my love
I never thought to see such a day
They said if you choose to disobey
What the comrades require,
You too will get the necklace of fire.
What has become of the children, my love,
The children, our children, my husband, my love?
They say that they will die for the cause,
But you, my love, you teach at the school
That they must obey the laws,
Therefore for you the comrades require
The necklace of fire.
They say you will get it tomorrow, my love,
Then what shall I do with the rest of my life,
Who am no longer a mother or wife,
But only a woman of sorrow?

Written while crossing the Atlantic in 1986
Unpublished

PRAISES AND ELEGIES

On the Death of J.H. Hofmeyr

Toll iron bell toll extolling bell
The toll is taken from the brave and the broken
Consoling bell toll
But toll the brave soul
Where no brave words are spoken

Strike iron bell strike ironic bell
Strike the bright name
From the dark scrolls
Of the blind nation
Strike sorrow strike shame
Into the blind souls

Clap iron bell clap iron clapper
Clap your iron hands together
Clap the loud applause
That life denied him
Clap the dead man
And if you can
The dead man's cause
Clap in beside him

Strike iron bell
Strike iron hammer
Strike deaf man's ears
Lest man's earth hears
Heaven's clanging and clamour

Clap iron bell clap iron clapper
And drown the clapping of the million million
Who clap the great batsman returning
To his Captain's pavilion

Anerley, 4 December 1948
The Forum, 1949

96

To Edgar Brookes

Tell me, What road are you going now?
  Have you considered its destination?
  Are your shoes stout enough?
  Does your heart pump blood?

Tell me, What words are you speaking now?
  Have you considered their meanings?
  Do you know that not all your wits
  Could make them return to your mouth?

Tell me, What men will go with you?
  Have you counted them? on one hand or two?
  Do you like hunger? and forced marches?
  Do you sleep well in the rain?

Tell me, What kind of cross do you want?
  Ebony? stinkwood? or chromium plated?
  That could be mass produced
  In cases of emergency?

  Do not trouble to report to me
  I know your answers already
  But when you report to the Lord
  Offer this pen with your sword.

Anerley, 1 February 1949
Unpublished

Praise Song for Luthuli

You there, Luthuli, they thought your world was small
They thought you lived in Groutville
Now they discover
It is the world you live in.

You there, Luthuli, they thought your name was small
Luthuli of Groutville
Now they discover
Your name is everywhere.

You there, Luthuli, they thought that you were chained
Like a backyard dog
Now they discover
They are in prison, but you are free.

You there, Luthuli, they took your name of Chief
You were not worthy
Now they discover
You are more Chief than ever.

Go well, Luthuli, may your days be long
Your country cannot spare you
Win for us also, Luthuli
The prize of Peace.

Durban, 5 December 1961
Knocking on the Door, 1975

Flowers for the Departed

Allison Krause, for you this flower
Desert-born in a distant land
Suddenly, in rain miraculous
Flamed into life and lit with orange fire
The arid plain. So may your seed,
Returned untimely to the earth
Bring back the beauty to your desert land.

Sandy Lee Sheuer, for you this flower
Shining and vivid like your life
Which fleeing as it were a shadow
Continued in so short a stay
May your shinningness return
To your dark land.

Jeffrey Miller for you this flower
A golden eye amidst a field of tares
Yet by the blind machine cut down
We mourn for you, and yet shall mourn
With ever-returning Spring.

William Schoeder, for you this last
From this far country.
Out of this grief come joy
Out of this darkness, light
Out of your dying, life.

America, for you these flowers
Would we could reach out hands to comfort you
But we dare not
We dare not touch those fingers dripping
With children's blood.

Botha's Hill, May 1970
New York Times, 1971

SONGS FROM THE MUSICAL MKHUMBANE

Opening Chorus

Mkhumbane, awake, awake, the day is soon to break
    and night is soon away.
Mkhumbane, Mkhumbane, there is no food for those who
    oversleep, oversleep
Wake for it is day.

Wake! for the city wakens too, and waits for the men
The men who work for Mother and child
    here in Mkhumbane.
Wake! for the buses waken too, to carry the men
The men who work for Mother and child
    here in Mkhumbane.

Mkhumbane, 1960

During rehearsal, May 1960: composer Todd Matshikiza at the piano, author Alan Paton leaning over
(extreme left) and director Malcolm Woolfson (behind the piano) with members of the choir.

Morning Song

Thousands and thousands and thousands are marching.
We come from the valleys of aloe and thorn.
Our feet walk the street of the town and the city.
This is the place where our children are born.

Good morning my brother
Morning my sister
No, I've got no time for talking
Can't you see how fast I'm walking?
'Morning. 'Morning.
Last time I was three minutes late,
The boss said 'boy we start at eight.
You come once more a minute past
And that once more will be your last.'

Phungula, what is this they say
That going home you lost your way.
They say you found the bridge too broad
And in the dark went overboard.
Ha, hahahahahaha!

Thousands and thousands and thousands are marching
On the road where the traveller cannot return.
Our feet walk the street of the town and the city.
These are the ways our children must learn.

Busman, wait a minute pray
Before you take my bread away.
Jobs are hard to get today

Busman, wait a minute pray.
Busman, half a minute pray
I told you what the people say:
Come just once more a minute past
And that once more will be your last.

Last night Mandela's child
was called away,

So long a journey
for so brief a stay.
Father, father be satisfied,
He is not the first that died.

Last night Mandela's wife was called away
So hard the labour for so little pay.
Husband, husband, be satisfied,
She is not the first that died.

Phungula, people say the river
Made you quake and shake and shiver,
But when your wife opened the door
You quaked and shaked and shivered more.
Ha, hahahahahaha!

Thousands and thousands and thousands are marching
On the road where the traveller cannot return.
Our feet walk the street of the town and the city.
These are the ways that our children must learn.

Mkhumbane, 1960

How the Enemy Ran!

Buthelezi's Song

I am myself an ordinary man
But people, I come from a famous clan
 How the enemy ran!
When our warrior song
Went rolling from hill to hill
 Mighty and strong
Every heart stood still
 In Zululand.

Ears cannot hear but memory can
The sounds of the place of my father's clan
 How the rivers ran!
From the forests the waterfalls
 Shout all the day
And hark how Bobini calls
 Ringing and gay
 In Zululand.

Brave and foolish the man
Who challenged my father's clan
 How the red blood ran!
How the assegai sped
Through the singing air
It was only the dead
Who would wait for us there
 In Zululand.

You men of the city beware
You heard what I said
It was only the dead
Who would wait for us there.
I myself am an ordin'ry man
But I come from a famous clan
And you will run as the enemy ran
 In Zululand.

Mkhumbane, 1960

Children's Song

The bell it rings for you and me,
Come girls, come boys, come all.
Come learn to take your place in life
When you are big and tall.

The whole world's waiting for you and for me,
Come pick and come pick and come pick what you'll be.

See now I close my eyes and look what I shall pick
I pick to be a nurse, and nurse you when you're sick.

The bell it rings for you and me,
Come girls, come boys, come all.
Come pick, come pick what you will be,
When you are grown and tall.

Come you and let us see what you will pick to be.

When I am grown and tall,
I pick a judge to be.
The rich man and the poor
Shall be the same to me.

The bell it rings for you and me,
Come girls, come boys, come all.
But what will you be, will you be, will you be,
When you are grown and tall.

Come you and let us see what you will pick to be.

I pick to be a singer
More than anything.
Perhaps one day the world
Will come to hear me sing.

The bell it rings for you and me,
Come girls, come boys, come all.
Come tell us, come tell us what you will be
When you are grown and tall.

Come you and let us see what you will pick to be.

I pick a policeman's lot,
It is a happy one.
Children will hold my hand
And only crooks will run.

The bell it rings for you and me,
Come girls, come boys, come all.
Come learn to take your place in life
When you are big and tall.

Mkhumbane, 1960

He's Looking for Work

He's looking,
    looking
        looking for work.

Won't take him long
    With his father's name,
Buthelezi,
    Buthelezi,
        Buthelezi.

Won't take him long
With that honest name.
Won't take him long
With that father's name,
Buthelezi,
    Buthelezi,
        Buthelezi.

That name Buthelezi,
It's fine and it's strong.
With that name Buthelezi
It can't take him long.

Mkhumbane, 1960

106

Factory Medley

Where are your papers? Your papers? Your papers?
　　Here is a man who is looking for work.
　　　No more today, come back tomorrow,
No more today.

Where are your papers? Your papers? Your papers?
　　　Where were you born? Where were you born?
　　　Who is your chief? Where was your home?
　　　Here is a boy who is looking for work.
　　　　No more today, come back tomorrow.
No more today.

You must be patient, you must be patient, you must follow
　　the rules,
　　　Where were you born? Who is your chief?
　　　Where was your home?
You must be patient, you must be patient,
These things take time.

Where are your papers? Your papers? Your papers?

Chorus:
Papers are important.
Papers are needed in this world.
If a child is born or an old one dies,
Papers are important.
But most of all to live . . . to work . . .
Papers are important.
These you must have.

Back and forth, back and forth,
To and fro, to and fro.
Au! I'm tired . . . tired . . . tired.

But I'll go back and forth, back and forth,
To and fro, to and fro
To look for papers,
Papers are important.
These you must have.

Mkhumbane, 1960

Tsotsi Song

We are the ones
That they talk about
When you come home
In the bus alone . . .
Who are those fellows
There at the back?

You kept the laws
And you gave no cause
For Death to come . . .
So sharp, so soon.
Your brow is wet
With sudden sweat . . .
Who are those fellows
There at the back?

Oh we are gay
We joke and play
Surely it can't
Be true what they say
If the dark night
Fills you with fright . . .

Mkhumbane, 1960

Who Will You Marry?

We're the boys with the smart turn-out,
We're the ones that they all talk about.
Don't you worry brother, don't take fright,
Our only fault is that we work at night.
It may be dang'rous brother joining us,
But leaving us may be more dangerous.
Don't be frightened, oh don't go away,
Don't believe all the things they say.

We're the girls of the Ship Shape Shop,
Someone must work or the world would stop.
Don't seem natural, and don't seem right
Married to a man who's out all night.
Think of the worries, think of the cares,
A woman she loves the children she bears.
Of all the jobs that are under the sun,
This is the job can't be done by one.

Who will you marry if you don't marry us?
Will you find honest men in some other city then?
Or find a decent stranger sitting next you in the bus?
Who will you marry if you do not marry us?

Who will we marry if we don't marry you?
How grievous and how heavy our troubles if we do,
A long day of weeping and a long night of rue,
But who will we marry if we do not marry you?

Who will you marry if you don't marry us?
Are we not the children of Mother Mkhumbane?
Did not many of your mothers also mother us?
Who will you marry if you do not marry us?

Who will we marry if we don't marry you?
For if we want to marry, it takes not one but two.
So if we want to marry what else can we do?
Who will we marry if we do not marry you?

Who will you marry if you don't marry us?
We play the same games and bear the same names.
And your fathers fathered us.
Who will you marry if you do not marry us?

Oh! Who will we marry if we don't marry you?
For some of us are foolish and don't mind what we do.
Your mothers and our mothers did the same as we will do.
Oh! Who will we (you) marry if we (you) do not marry you
    (us)?

Mkhumbane, 1960

But Now They Don't Laugh Any More

Mr Charlemagne's Song

I'm really quite good at remembering names
There's hardly one that escapes me.
Just cross my path and see what I mean
You'll see my memory's evergreen
From January to the end of December
I don't forget to remember.

I remember they laughed when I was poor
But now they don't laugh any more
For in the end I got to the top
And have a place like the Ship Shape Shop
I have riches and I have fame
Everyone knows Charlemagne is the name.

Charlemagne! Charlemagne!
Everyone knows Charlemagne is the name!
Let them hear it again and again
Charlemagne! Charlemagne!

Lady, what can I show you today?
We can sell whatever you say,
Nylons and socks
And the latest in frocks
We sell fish and we sell meats
We sell sugar and we sell sweets
We sell butter and we sell flour
We sell might and we sell power
How they laughed when I was poor
But now they don't laugh any more.

Chorus:
He can sell whatever you say,
Nylons and socks
And the latest in frocks
He sells fish and he sells meats
He sells sugar and he sells sweets
He sells butter and he sells flour
He sells might and he sells power
How they laughed when he was poor
But now they don't laugh any more.

Mkhumbane, 1960

Young Love

The world is full of change and woe
Some say it always will be so
But not for me
My love is steadfast as a star
Though you be near or you be far
My love will be where'soever you are
That's where my love will be.

Old people they are very wise
They say that love is sorrow
You hear them say
Forget today
There's always a tomorrow
But as for me
My love will be
The same today, tomorrow.

They say we are too young to know
They say that we should part
They say time heals a broken heart
And comfort brings for every loss
They make me cross
I think when people live too long
They see the world all wrong
They should leave grave decisions
To those with younger visions.

Oh yes the world is full of woe
I guess that it was always so
This is the price one pays
For all the joys of living
In my tomorrow
I do not ask
That we be spared all sorrow
All stormy weather
I only ask
We face it both together.

Mkhumbane, 1960

112

Song
Rachel's Lament

Child, why did you come to me?
Why did you come to show me
The kind of child I used to be
And send me back to weeping?

Child, why did you come to me?
Bring back the past to me?
Why did you come to wake my heart
That was grown used to sleeping?

Oh boy from home
Who sleeps in the bitter sea,
Why does time take so long to go by?
Oh boy from home
Who sleeps in the bitter sea,
Do not look at me now,
So old, so careless am I.

Now for a day or two
I'll be what I used to be,
For the sake of these tender two
Who remind me of you and me.
So girl with the wonderful boy
I'm glad you came to me

Mkhumbane, 1960

113

Bantustan

Lady, won't you look at us
Jack
and Dick
and Dan,
and Gus,
Lady, won't you choose a man
There's Gus and Jack and Dick and Dan,
Won't you make a marrying plan?

I have no plan to take a man,
Gus and Jack and Dick and Dan,
But if I should make such a plan
I'd want a man who was a man
I'd want a man from Bantustan.

Lady don't decide so quick
There's Gus and Jack and Dan and Dick
A nice little house Kwa Mashu way
Perhaps a nice little car one day.

Oh Gus and Jack and Dan and Dick
I haven't made up my mind so quick
But for city slickers I don't care
I want a man of the open air
I want a man who will and can
I want a man from Bantustan.

Lady it's very dangerous
Say Jack and Dick and Dan and Gus
What if he feeds you on bark and roots?
What if he goes to bed in his boots?

Jack and Dick and Dan and Gus
I don't think it's so dangerous
What if he feeds me on bark and roots?
What if he goes to bed in his boots?
So long as he loves me like a man
And that means a man from Bantustan.

Lady why not a city man
Gus or Jack or Dick or Dan?
Lady be kind, lady be fair
We're not *afraid* of the open air.

Gus and Jack, and Dick and Dan,
I was once in love with a city man
He wouldn't go out in the open air
Without his woollen underwear
I said to him I love you man
But I'd love you better in Bantustan.

Bantustan, Bantustan,
That's where a man can be a man
And when I make a marrying plan
It'll be a man who is a man
It'll be a man who will and can
It'll be a man from Bantustan.

Mkhumbane, 1960

115

Be Satisfied

Catherine's Song

This night a mother's son is called away
So long a journey for so short a stay
Mother, mother, be satisfied
He is not the first that died.

This night a young girl's love is called away
So sweet, so brief, the flower of a day
Lover, lover, be satisfied
He is not the first that died.

So sweet, so brief, the flower of a day
Up with the sun and with the sun away
People, people be satisfied
He is not the first that died.

Mkhumbane, 1960

Closing Song

Mkhumbane, it's time for sleep, it's time for eyes to close,
    From troubles of the day.
Mkhumbane, Mkhumbane, there is no food for those who
    oversleep, oversleep,
Sleep then while you may.

Sleep, for the city's sleeping too, and quietness lies
Like tender hand on sleeping eyes
    Here in Mkhumbane.
Sleep, for the long day's work is done, and darkness is come
To bring it's sleep to every home
    Here in Mkhumbane.

Mkhumbane, 1960

116

FOURTH JOURNEY

SPIRITUAL EXERCISES

MEDITATIONS

Faith

I see with passing of the tragic years
Children made fatherless, mothers forgot
By those whose liberty was bought with theirs,
What time the Author of the shining spheres
Stands leagues aloof from their unhappy lot
Till He sends Death upon them unawares.

I see the tott'ring of man's house of faith.
They flee for refuge to their man-made law
Unwitting of its birth of their own lust.
A vain security that's but a wraith
Hiding a moment the red tooth and claw
That makes us beasts and chains us to the dust.

I hear the welling warmth of chants and creeds
Fashioned by men and hallowed by belief.
I hear the welling deepness of the notes
Of some cathedral organ. Wind in reeds,
The same our pagan sires on some wild reef
Heard and held captive in their pagan throats.

I hear the poignant valour of their hymns
To unknown Gods within their hallowed place,
Songs of despair sung on a darkling shore.
A torch of faith that spurts and wanes and dims
Casting its paleness on each wasted face
Leaving the darkness darker than before.

There comes to me a vision of the end
Distorted in the chaos of my mind
Fouling my sleep and catching at my breath.
Burn out my eyes, but pity will not send
That my imagination be as blind.
No hand can still it but the hand of death.

The suns glow redly in the universe,
And in the gloom the earth's miscegenates
Learn at their mothers' knees in nameless fright
How once before the coming of the Curse
The days were glitt'ring jewellery, and spates
Of yellow stars adorned the pall of night.

Legend is all that lives of peace and wars,
Men crash their murd'rous way for human food
Like carnivores through jungles of the past.
And ruined cities silent on the shores
Of dying seas, hive in their sewers the brood
Of man-faced rodents, Evolution's last.

I marvel in the foul faeces of Doom
That some kill not nor eat the flesh of man,
A dwindling brotherhood bound by their vow.
Whose children in this horror-pit of gloom
Reach manhood safely, even to the span
Of three and thirty years, man's measure now.

A dwindling brotherhood that men call Christ's,
Who travel unafraid the streets, and with
Curses and yells are murdered as they go.
And keep in some old ruin faithful trysts
Talking with shining faces of some myth
Someone who died a million years ago.

Pietermaritzburg, 27 September 1931
Natal University College Magazine, 1931

(See Notes at the end for further references to the various poems)

119

Meditation for a Young Boy Confirmed

I

I rise from my dream, and take suddenly this pen and this paper
For I have seen with my eyes a certain beloved person, who lives in a
distant country,
I have seen hands laid upon him, I have heard the Lord asked to
defend him,
I have seen him kneel with trust and reverence, and the innocence of
him smote me in the inward parts.
I remembered him with most deep affection, I regarded him with
fear and with trembling,
For life is waiting for him, to wrest the innocence from his young
boy's eyes,
So I write urgently for this beloved person, and indeed for all
beloved persons,
I write indeed for any person, whoever may find something in
these words.

II

I see him there young and very innocent, he still confides many
things to many persons,
I know what is waiting for him, I see enemies and dragons and
apparitions,
I know them all, I am familiar with them, I walk amongst them
carelessly,
I walk amongst them having a truce with them, but I cannot make
a truce with them for any other person,
I cannot make a truce with them for any young and reverent person,
nor any gentle child;
Therefore though I myself walk through them carelessly, today
they fill me with most anxious trembling.

III

My son writes to me, Today I made my first communion,
I was rather nervous, but everything went off satisfactorily.
I see him communicating, I observe that he believes himself to be
in the presence of the One and Everlasting and Most Loving God,
I observe him at the altar rails, I observe his heart is beating,

I observe that he is anxious to behave correctly, I know that he will
    blush if he makes some error,
I observe that he stretches out his hands, that he partakes of the
    bread and wine,
I observe that he returns to his place, that he casts down his eyes
    and does not look about him.

IV

I watch him with old and knowledgeable and very old eyes, I am
    aware that he has been indoctrinated,
I am aware that his choice is contingent, that I have allowed him
    to commit himself deeply,
I am aware that he is neither a Buddhist nor a Muslim, that his
    circumstances have hardly permitted him to consider these religions.
I am aware that the whole world is not confirmed, that the whole
    world does not communicate,
I am aware that some climate has changed in the world, therefore
    I write these words to him.

V

I say to my son, These are the visible and outward forms,
These are the inarticulate gestures, the humble and supplicating
    hands of the blind reached out,
This is the reaching out of children's hands for the wild bird, these are
    the hands stretched out for water in the dry and barren land.
This is the searching in a forest for a treasure, buried long since
    under a tree with branches,
This is the searching in the snowstorm for the long-waited letter,
    the lost white paper that has blown away,
This is the savage seeking a tune from the harp, the man raking
    the ashes for the charm in the burned-down house.
This is man thrusting his head through the stars, searching the void
    for the Incomprehensible and Holy;
Keep for it always your reverence and earnestness, these are men
    searching here,
They stretch out their hands for no star, for no knowledge however
    weighty,
They reach out humbly, supplicating, not more than a cubit's length
That haply they may touch the hem of the robe of the Infinite and
    Everlasting God.

VI

This kneeling, this singing, this reading from ancient books,
This acknowledgement that the burden is intolerable, this promise
    of amendment,
This humble access, this putting out of the hands,
This taking of the bread and wine, this return to your place not
    glancing about you,
This solemn acceptance and the thousand sins that will follow it,
    this thousand sins and the repenting of them,
This dedication and this apostasy, this apostasy and this restoration,
This thousand restorations and this thousand apostasies,
Take and accept them all, be not affronted nor dismayed by them.
They are a net of holes to capture essence, a shell to house the
    thunder of an ocean,
A discipline of petty acts to catch Creation, a rune of words to hold
    One Living Word,
A Ladder built by men of sticks and stones, whereby they hope to
    reach to heaven.

VII

You will observe that virgins do not bear children, and that dead
    men are not resurrected;
You will read in the newspapers of wars and disasters, but they will
    report miracles with impatience.
You will be distressed, you will not wish to repudiate your
    commitment,
You will not wish to disappoint your parents, you will suffer deep
    troubling of the soul,
You will cry out like David before you, My God, my God, why hast
    thou forsaken me?
Do not hastily concede this territory, do not retreat immediately,
Pass over the slender bridges, pick your road quickly through the
    marshes,
Observe the frail planks left by your predecessors, the stones gained
    only by leaping;
Press on to the higher ground, to the great hills and the mountains
From whose heights men survey the eternal country, and the city
    that has no need of moon or sun.
But do not lie to yourself, admit this is the journey of the heart.

VIII

Listen to my opinion, accept or reject it.
The intellect is like a searchlight, it probes the darkness to and fro
    unceasingly,
Its rays at their limit describe a great sphere, and this is the universe
    of the intellect,
But this is not the universe of God, and God is not captured in it.
We do not search the darkness for him, and pronounce that he is
    not there,
Nor do we hold him caught in the beam, and declare him to be
    exposed and humbled.
Our intellect is of finite glory, but God is of Infinite Glory;
It cannot make or unmake the Creator, it is he who created it.
It can rebel, but it is a proud and desolate rebellion;
We may yet fly to the stars, we may yet fire our guns and wake to
    echoing the waste mountains of long-dead places,
But all that we do shall be of the order of what is done already,
    our searchlights fall back from the edge of the outermost void,
They fall back, they are exhausted, who shall make them rise higher?
Shall we say of the intellect, we shall devise means to exalt it?
Shall we say of our created nature, we shall otherwise create it?
No, we must say to the poets and to the humble, what moves in the
    outermost void?

IX

Do not pronounce judgement on the Infinite, nor suppose God to
    be like a bad Prime Minister,
Do not suppose him powerless, or if powerful malignant,
Do not address your mind to criticism of the Creator, do not pretend
    to know his categories,
Do not take his Universe in your hand, and point out its defects
    with condescension.
Do not think he is a greater potentate, a manner of President of
    the United Galaxies,
Do not think that because you know so few human beings, that he
    is in a comparable though more favourable position.
Do not think it absurd that he should know every sparrow, or the
    number of the hairs of your head,
Do not compare him with yourself, nor suppose your human love
    to be an example to shame him.

123

He is not greater than Plato or Lincoln, nor superior to Shakespeare
and Beethoven,
He is their God, their powers and their gifts proceeded from him,
In infinite darkness they poured with their fingers over the first word
of the Book of his Knowledge.

X

This is not reason, men do call it faith.
If ten men came to me, now some I should confound, and by some
be confounded,
And those I do confound shall leave me for an easier victory,
And those that me confounded shall find elsewhere defeat.
And who, to God found in an argument, will put out supplicating
hands?
I do not lie to you, I tell you plainly,
I do not presume to bring my knowledge into his presence, I go
there humbly.
All this I recommend to you, it is the heart of worship.

XI

Such was the brief, such was the lonely life,
Such was the bondage of the earth, such was the misery,
Such was the reaching out, such was the separation,
That my Lord tore the curtain from the skies, and in compassion
He took upon himself all angry things, the scourge, the thorn, the nail,
the utter separation;
And spoke such words as made me tremble, and laid his yoke upon me
And bound me with these chains, that I have worn with no especial
grace.
Why then I did accept this miracle, and being what I am some lesser
miracles,
And then I did accept this Faith, and being what I am some certain
Articles,
And then I did accept this Law, and being what I am some
regulations,
Why then I worshipped him, and being what I am knelt in some pew
And heard some organ play and some bells peal, and heard some
people sing,
And heard about some money that was wanted, and heard some sin
was preached against,

And heard some message given by some man, sometimes with great
　　distinction, sometimes with none.
I made this humble access, I too stretched out my hands,
Sometimes I saw him not, and sometimes clearly, though with my
　　inward eyes.
I stayed there on my knees, I saw his feet approaching,
I saw the mark of the nails, I did not dare to look fully at them,
I longed to behold him, I did not dare to behold him,
I said in my heart to him, I who in sins and doubts and in my grievous
　　separation reach out my hands,
Reach out your hands and touch me, O most Holy One.

　　XII
I see my son is wearing long trousers, I tremble at this;
I see he goes forward confidently, he does not know so fully his own
　　gentleness.
Go forward, eager and reverent child, see here I begin to take my
　　hands away from you,
I shall see you walk careless on the edges of the precipice, but if you
　. wish you shall hear no word come out of me;
My whole soul will be sick with apprehension, but I shall not disobey you.
Life sees you coming, she sees you come with assurance towards her,
She lies in wait for you, she cannot but hurt you;
Go forward, go forward, I hold the bandages and ointments ready,
And if you would go elsewhere and lie alone with your wounds, why
　　I shall not intrude upon you,
If you would seek the help of some other person, I shall not come
　　forcing myself upon you.

　　XIII
If you should fall into sin, innocent one, that is the way of this
　　pilgrimage;
Struggle against it, not for one fraction of a moment concede its
　　dominion.
It will occasion you grief and sorrow, it will torment you,
But hate not God, nor turn from him in shame or self-reproach;
He has seen many such, his compassion is as great as his Creation.
Be tempted and fall and return, return and be tempted and fall
A thousand times and a thousand, even to a thousand thousand.
For out of this tribulation there comes a peace, deep in the soul and
　　surer than any dream,

And in the old and knowledgeable eyes there dwells, perhaps, some
    child's simplicity
That even asks for gifts and prays for sons.

XIV

Listen to one more word from me, now that I begin to take my hands
    from you.
Now God be thanked for this so brief possession, so full of joy,
This zest for life, this keen anticipation of some quite trivial thing,
This ingenuity for making occupations, these programmes strictly
    adhered to,
This typewriter sadly out of gear, on which were thundered out
    messages, poems, plays, and proclamations,
These rages, these lunatic stampings, these threats of leaving home,
For these withdrawals of affection, when you sat pouting like a pigeon,
For these restorations, at all costs to be accepted gravely, even with
    penitence,
For this reverence, this eagerness, this confidence in many persons,
For all these gifts we give our thanks.

XV

I see him communicating, I observe that he believes himself to be in
    the presence of the One and Everlasting and Most Loving God,
I observe that he goes to the altar rails, I observe his heart is beating,
I observe that he is anxious to behave correctly, I know he will blush if
    he makes some error,
I observe his humble access, his putting out of his hands,
I observe that he returns to his place, not glancing about him, I watch
    him with old and knowledgeable and very old eyes,
I say to myself, So would I wish to communicate.

XVI

I put my pen down, round me the world is dark and all men lie asleep.
But I have written urgently for this beloved person, and indeed for all
    beloved persons
I have written urgently for this my son, and for all sons and daughters,
And indeed for any person, whoever may find something in these words.

Lane's Flat, January 1950
The Christian Century, 1954

126

PSALMS AND DEVOTIONAL VERSE

No Place for Adoration

I saw the famous gust of wind in Eloff Street
It came without notice, shaking the blinds and awnings
Ten thousand people backed to the wall to let it pass
And all Johannesburg was awed and silent,
Save for an old prostitute woman, her body long past pleasure
Who ran into the halted traffic, holding up hands to heaven
And crying my Lord and my God, so that the whole city laughed
This being no place for adoration.

Lane's Flat, 3 December 1949
Knocking on the Door, 1975

My Lord has a great attraction . . .

My Lord has a great attraction for the humble and simple,
they delight in his conversation,

The insane stop their frenzies and look at him unsurely,
then they crowd round him and finger him gently,

Their wistful eyes capture something that was lost, they
are healed for a moment of the hurts of great institutions.

The half-witted press their simple thoughts upon him, and
he listens with attention to the babbling of imbeciles.

He knows their meanings, and they observe him trustfully.

He passes through the great gates of Alcatraz, and there is
no searching machine that can prevent him,

He goes into the cells that have the iron doors, where the
wild men are shut in completely,

They put their wild teeth on his hands, but take them away
again from his wounds with wonder.

Oh Lord teach us your wisdom, and incline our hearts to
receive your instructions.

Then the maniac would stay his hands from the small girl,
and the drunken man from the throat of the woman,

And the father his hands from the growing son, and the son
his hands from the father.

And the wild boys could be brought out from the cages, and
the wild men from behind the unutterable doors.

Lane's Flat, 13 December 1949
South African Outlook, 1953

128

What is this sound . . .

What is this sound from the world? These voices I hear?
It is women and children crying, and even men
From all the cities of earth, and every country,
Behind their locks and their bolts they cry for their fear.

It is the lamentation and the crying
Of men that are afraid of men, afraid
Each of himself, of sleeping and of rising,
Of being born, of living and of dying.

It is not always seen, they make their faces
Into the moulds of smiles but their eyes are unsmiling
They move from place to place that they need not be still
And captive move to other captive places.

They flock to the coasts and lie there under the sky
They lie in deep lush grass by singing waters
They lie on slopes of mountains under the sun
But nothing comes to them, where'er they lie.

They put caressing hands on boles of trees
And pick some small sweet flower to console them
And walk with naked feet on stones of streams
But there is nothing comes to them from these.

Possibly Lane's Flat, 13 December 1949
Unpublished and untitled

A Psalm of the Forest

I have seen my Lord in the forest, He walks from tree to tree
    laying His hands upon them.
The yellowwoods stand upright and proud that He comes amongst
    them, the chestnut throws down blooms at His feet.
The thorns withdraw their branches before Him, they will not
    again be used shamefully against Him.
The wild fig makes a shade for Him, and no more denies Him.
The monkeys chatter and skip about in the branches, they peer
    at Him from behind their fingers,
They shower Him with berries and fruits, they shake the owls
    and the nightjars from their hiding places,
They stir the whole forest, they screw up their faces,
They say to each other unceasingly, it is the Lord.
The mothers cuff their children, and elder brothers the younger,
But they jump from tree to tree before Him, they bring down
      the leaves like rain,
Nothing can bring them to order, they are excited to see the Lord.
And the winds move in the upper branches, they dash them like
    cymbals together,
They gather from all the four corners, and the waterfalls shout
    and thunder,
The whole forest is filled with roaring, with an acknowledgement,
    an exaltation.

Lane's Flat, 18 December 1949
South African Outlook, 1953

Heavy with secret knowledge . . .

Heavy with secret knowledge the earth turns
And in its Edens dangerous fruit
Ripens. Naked again, man shrinks from the blast
Of the extra-galactic winds, and would return
To Time's womb, and curl himself
In the warmth of lost simplicity
If he but could. But there's no returning.

The telephone wires of the outer void
Shrill in the gales, God's voice
Speaking urgently to a frightened race
That He has not lost compassion.
Bare your breast, humanity
And take the jarring impulses
Into the heart again.

For what did my Lord die? So that the earth
Could finally incredulous and faithless utterly
Make past event of present grace?
So that man's knowledge could parallel Creation
And send a star into the void again?
That's not my reckoning.

Shall the physician in a healing frenzy
Thrust his knife into the helpless heart,
And the engineer build such a bridge
That all mankind could walk on it
And go helpless down to death
In a last San Luis Rey?

No knowledge have I in my brain
That can match such answering,
Only the knowledge that all's sustained
And moves not from its ordination
Without the flicker of God's eye
In the divine permission.

Fearful, I have no fear. My life
Lies in God's Hand, cupped, intact,
But that He touches it. My spirit
That is His breath on dust
Goes back into His mouth when he inspires.
I have no being otherwise
And do not tremble for my dust.

Is the earth dead, and the great meanings
Of the great event perished like rubber
So that none may dare to stretch them out
To cover us again, and despair
Because the hand that holds the pen
And brush and knife, so no sight or sound
Can move us longer?

Ah then I'd dare being not daring
To trumpet forth the high estate of man
Being God's making, and show his face
In a mirror, that he might see
Out of his bold or frightened eyes
The forgotten image.

Undated, but probably Lane's Flat, 19 December 1949
Unpublished and untitled

For the earth is corrupted . . .

For the earth is corrupted, even the leaf and the stone
Sad sad is the earth and terrible now men's home
And hoping brings no hope and knowledge no knowing
And the old ones sit in the sun and wait to be gone.

And who wish well to the sire and dam of a birth
They greet with sorrowful eyes the new-come child
And under the puling cries they hear insistent and deep
The dark and desolate dirge of man's home and the earth.

Lane's Flat, probably the end of December 1949
Unpublished and untitled

Oh Lord, my enemies overwhelm me ...

Oh Lord, my enemies overwhelm me, they make me ashamed
by their taunts,

They say thou art remote from us, that the earth is
only thy jest.

They shout it out in the market-places, they whisper
it in the churches,

Their scientists state it baldly, but their theologians
clothe it in tresses of platinum and gold.

Oh Lord, be not silent, nor hold any more thy peace;

Cry out from the heavens, beware to be remote from the Lord.

The vengeance of the Lord is terrible, he will let them
build a ladder to heaven,

He will permit them to walk there like gods, and to
open his cupboards discourteously.

He will tempt them in his wrath, and let them find
the flash of his anger
That can shatter the rocks and the water, and bring
the earth to destruction.

But if they make a God of their knowledge, and are
contemptuous of compassion

He will strike them down utterly, and darkness
shall rule again the face of the deep.

Lane's Flat, probably the end of December, 1949
Unpublished and untitled

134

PRAYERS

O Lord give me that grace . . .

O Lord give me that
grace that I may so
   carry myself, and the
courage that I may so
bear up myself, as
    that I may fear none
    but thee, and nothing but
    that wherein I offend
    thee, even for
    J.C.'s sake Amen

January, 1953
Unpublished and untitled

Prayer

For the use of one in authority
(Written for a Kent Headmaster)

My plan be in Thy mind, O God
My work be in Thy hands
My ears be ever swift to hear
The words of Thy commands.

My feet be ever swift to run
When I am called by Thee
My hands be ever swift to do
The task Thou givest me.

O may my weak and earth-blind eyes
Be ever swift to see
Thine image in each son of Thine
Thou dost commit to me.

Dwell Thou in every hall and room
In every head and heart
Walk Thou the roads and fields of Kent
That Kent be where Thou art.

Be pleased the bounty of Thy grace
On this Thy School to pour
As Thou hast done these fifty years
Do Thou these fifty more.

Written in 1955
Kent Quarterly, 1989

A Daily Prayer for One's Work

O God my Maker, from whom all my gifts proceed,
I pray earnestly that You will help me to use them.
Remove from me all sloth, uncertainty, vanity,
self-satisfaction, and fear, that might hinder me
in my work.

Help me to be industrious, and help me to continue
working even when the work seems poor. I do not ask
to be saved from melancholy, but I ask the strength
to get up and do something, for You and others and
myself, when I am fallen into it.

And help me to struggle continually to think more of
others and less of myself. Lord listen to my prayer.
Amen.

Botha's Hill, 17 January, 1972
Unpublished

FIFTH JOURNEY

INDULGENCES

HUMOUR AND SATIRE

"No responsibility accepted.".....Ed.

Ho, Long One, what do you do?
I build, Master, with wattle and mud,
And finished, lie me down in the sun
And watch my toes lift, one by one,
That's what I do.

Ho! ho! Long One, that's what you do.
Your fathers built with spear and blood,
And you, ho! ho! with wattle and mud,
That's what you do.

Laugh well, White One, you laugh to-day.
Tomorrow we build the white man's way,
Tomorrow, Master, what'll you say?

Tomorrow, dog, will be as to-day.
Think you to walk where the white man walks?
Think you to talk as the white man talks?
Think's all you'll do.

Tomorrow, Master, will be as to-day,
Tomorrow the same — in a different way,
Your best, our best, will lie in the sun,
And watch *our* toes lift, one by one
That's what we'll do.

Natal University College Magazine, 1929

(See Notes at the end for further references to the various poems)

The Hermit

I have barred the doors
Of the place where I bide,
I am old and afraid
Of the world outside.

How the poor souls cry
In the cold and the rain,
I have blocked my ears,
They shall call me in vain.

If I peer through the cracks
Hardly daring draw breath,
They are waiting there still
Patient as death.

The maimed and the sick
The tortured of soul,
Arms outstretched as if
I could help them be whole.

No shaft of the sun
My hiding shall find,
Go tell them outside
I am deaf, I am blind.

Who will drive them away,
Who will ease me my dread,
Who will shout to the fools
"He is dead! he is dead"!

Sometimes they knock
At the place where I hide,
I am old, and afraid
Of the world outside.

Do they think, do they dream
I will open the door?
Let the world in
And know peace no more?

Pietermaritzburg, 22 March 1931
Natal University College Magazine, 1931

My Sense of Humour

My friends are angry with me
Because I have lost
My sense of humour.

They remind me of occasions
When I have had the room rolling
With my wit.

They weep with despair
Over my sorrowful book
And sombre verses.

Well I too have pondered
This sad matter
With regret.

The truth is I have struggled
To get my humour
Into its harness.

But it bucks like a beast
And rears and kicks and will not get
Between the shafts.

I have a suspicion
It does not like the strange carriage
I am driving.

I feel like saying to it
I do not like it either.
Obey, like myself.

Anerley, 11 October 1948
Knocking on the Door, 1975

The Chief

Alone I sit upon the hollow throne,
The Thunderer whose thunder's hollow, Chief
And King no better than king's fool, with brief
Heart-rotten majesty, whose shame is known
To every supplicant, though I alone
Ruling with gutless pomp the hollow fief
Know it most deeply to the depths of grief.
The desolate, the desert, and the stone.
The children taught by mothers from their birth
Of my swift justice, and of how the earth
Shook when I walked, so flaunt their painted lips
And smoke their cigarettes and jive their hips
About me that I now rebukeless go
All through them silent, knowing that they know.

Anerley, November 1948
Unpublished

The Joke

Let me relate a small affair.
A room. Johannesburg. Ten of us there.
One said, don't think that I presume
But if a bomb fell on this room
Why that would end the liberal cause.
Oh my the laughs! the loud guffaws!

Why, even now, I choke
Over that joke.

New York, 11 November 1949
Knocking on the Door, 1975

Once in the Tavern . . .

Once in the Tavern of the Seas
The penguin and the phalarope
Did meet and of their joy imbibe
Some real Cape Province dope.

Thus quite unusually they spoke
With forthright tongues and free
And said what never they'd have said
Just ordinarily.

'I'm sick and tired,' the penguin said,
'Of ice and snow, in future
I'm spending all my winter vacs
Up there at Cape St Lucia.'

And then the gentle phalarope
He too was sick of ice and snow
And thought he'd spend his winter vac
Up there at Ermelo.

At Ermelo, the penguin said
'My God you go too far
My God we are both ocean birds
Let's stick to what we are.'

'And who are you,' said phalarope
'My God, sir, who are you?
I'll go to any bloody place
To make that book come true.'

Letter to Neville Nuttall, 12 September, 1951
Unpublished and untitled

My Great Discovery

After much exploratory
Work in my laboratory
I made an epoch-making
Breath-taking
Discovery.

Can you not picture me?
Can you not see me there,
Wild eyes, disordered hair,
With fanatical persistence
And white-robed assistants
In masks,
And flasks
Smoking, choking
Everywhere?

I cannot give to such as you
The reasoning which led me to
This epoch-making
Breath-taking
Discovery.

For if you look
At all the poems in this book
You will observe that I have undertaken
And have so far remained unshaken
In my quite revolutionary plan
To write so that the common man
May understand.
Therefore I cannot give to you
The reasoning which led me to
My great discovery.

Well, this discovery
Was simple as could be
Five straight injections
Position, lumbar
In colour, umber
Taste, very like cucumber
Effect, inducing slumber
And if I may remind you
Five in number —
These five injections could erase
In just as many days
The pigmentation
From any nation.

I sat astounded
Completely dumbfounded
By the epoch-making
Breath-taking
Discovery.
Being a scientist, delighted
Being South African, affrighted
In Great Britain, knighted.
I seized the telephone
And in a voice unlike my own
(Not through dissembling
But through trembling)
Government, I said
The girl said, what division?
I said, no divisions any more.

She said, I mean what section?
I said, no sections any more.
She said, I'll report you,
(Or deport you,
I can't quite say
I am not au fait
With recent legislation)
I said, you go ahead
Or I shall plunge the nation
Into a conflagration.
I know that shocked her
She said, you need the Doctor
I said, yes get the Doctor
And all the Cabinet,
For I can change the pigmentation
Of any nation.
To cut the story short
She gave a kind of snort
And got the real big Boss
Who said, of coss, of coss,
Come up at once.

It is no kind of pret
To face a Cabinet
They were astounded
And dumfounded.
One said, Good Lord
And hummed and hawed
And one was suave
Just like the papers say.
And one was gay
And said this is the day
For if the pigmentation
Of any nation
Can suffer alteration
Why the whole fact of race
Takes on another face.
But another Minister
Looking quite sinister
Just like the papers say

Said this suggestion
Requires digestion
Let's meet another day.

And so again I met
The Cabinet
And this same Minister
Still looking sinister
Said, does this alteration
Of the pigmentation
Of any nation,
Just work from black to white
Or do you think it might
Change also white to black?
And I replied
All full of pride
The recipe can be supplied
For any shade
In beige or jade
In snow or jet
Or violet.
Then sir, he said, I here submit
A list of those to be
Changed with this recipe.
He pushed the list across
To the big Boss
My eyes are fine
A shiver went right down my spine
The leading name was mine.

I reached into my pocket
And pressed the radar switch
That sent the radar rocket
Which
Blew up the laboratory
And all work exploratory
Plus my assistants
Whom at this distance

I spared the degradation
The gross humiliation
Of working for a caitiff
Who had gone naitiff.

Probably written in 1953
Africa South, 1957

Dr Verwoerd my boss . . .

Dr. Verwoerd my boss my boss
It really is for me imposs
To utter here my secret thoughts
But I am thinking lots and lots.

No words of mine can justice do
To you, my boss, my boss, to you
No words of mine can hope to say
What I am thinking, boss, today.

We read about your iron hand
And boss, we really understand
But boss I cannot here convey
The half of what we really say.

My boss, my boss, I hope and pray
Harder than I can really say
I pray that you will live to see
The end of all your industry.

Sent to Leslie Rubin, 13 September 1957
Unpublished and untitled

149

INFORMAL WRITINGS
OCCASIONAL VERSE

Hail to the Chief

I do not claim to be like Brookes
Although I may have better looks.
But now tonight I mean to show it
That he is not the only poet.
Each birthday party he brings verse
Which is sometimes bad and sometimes worse.
One verse he writes as Shakespeare would,
The next is in the style of Hood.
Poor Shelley next must then submit
To this display of misplaced wit.
I shall not emulate this feat,
This poem is my own complete.
However we congratulate
Edgar on his doctorate,
May he live long to wear the gown
And bring fresh lustre to his town.
You know from Cape Town to the Congo
Each Chieftain has his pet imbongo,
Who cries out praises on the spot
Whether they are deserved or not.
Alas imbongo have I none
So I have got a chief for one.
And from his distant northern fief
He comes to Botha's Hill this chief
And having heard imbongos many
He does not yield the palm to any.
And brave he is to come at all
His name, already low, will fall
Because it is already known
Thanks to that boon, the telephone,

That he is here with us tonight
Playing with fire and dynamite.
The fire is Hurley full of fight
And Edgar is the dynamite.
I thank you Gatsha nevertheless
Your eloquence and fine finesse
Even a dullard would impress.
And thank you Irene for coming as well
And telling Gatsha what to tell.
And we too wish you well great Chief
And peace and joy in your northern fief.

11 January, 1970
Read by Paton at his birthday party; unpublished

Prologue

To be spoken by a young person.

Unto us a child is born
That's the title of our play
Unto us a child is born
You will see that child today.

Do not look up at the sky
He is not that far away
He is with us here tonight
In the players and the play.

He is in the prisoner
He is in the halt and lame
He is in the sick, the poor,
Let us glorify His name.

And His spirit moves in us
When we help the halt and lame
You may not see you may not hear
But He's present all the same.

151

He's not caught in any creed
Nor in buildings made by men
When we give ourselves in love
He is present then.

Unto us a child is born
Worshipped, treasured and adored
That's the title of our play
Made for Him, our Friend and Lord.

Listen all that you may hear
What this Christmas story tells
Christ is born and Christ is risen
When His spirit in us dwells.

Written for Peter Stayt's Christmas play, 1968
Unpublished

For Ray Swart's Fiftieth Birthday

On this great historic date
We have come to celebrate
50 years of noble worth
Seldom seen upon the earth.

Ray of sunshine ray of light
Ray of brilliance infinite
Messenger from heaven sent
To shine again in Parliament.

Nats complain with grief and pain
Traitor Swart is back again
But we with heart and soul rejoice
To hear again that mighty voice.

February 1978
Unpublished

152

New Year's Eve 1982 at the Swarts'

Welcome all, to 1982
And I don't only mean the PFP
You must not let it trouble you
But I include P.W.
And I include — dis darem erg
Die groot bewoners van die Waterberg
And Jaap Marais and dear old Vause
Whose parties are in menopause
Rajbansi who has drawn the ire
Of old Ramesar's feeble fire
And Gatsha breathing threats and love
And brandishing his velvet glove.
The Matanzimas all smiles and charms
Not to mention a couple of farms
Mangope and Bophuthatswana
Richer today than poor old Ghana
Thanks to Sol and the Sun Hotels
And all the visiting guys and belles
Frank Sinatra and Liz Minelli
If only one could get Gene Kelley
To dance in the rain with Gary Player
What could be better, what could be gayer?
And a better New Year to the SABC
Though not exactly my cup of tea
I confess I'm driven nearly dippy
By the urbane smile of dear old Kim Shippey
And for the rest — Yarwell Nofine —
It sends a shiver right down your spine.
I grant one seldom gets the chance
To hear old Brezhnev speaking Afrikaans
Those racing drivers are very clever
I can watch them going round for ever
The same old corners, the same old bends
And alas! the same old sticky ends.
And I cannot wait for the dear old Artes
Drinking champagne and eating sosaties

So a good New Year to Sybil Hotz
For when the Moving Finger Tots
Up her account, she will be in the black
She something has that others lack.
And a good New Year to naughty Boesak
Though some would like tell him 'voe'sak'
Why must he go to Ottawa, Can?
Why can't he speak out here like a man?
Don't worry, friend Boesak, whatever they say
You've done a good thing for the NGK
And now it's time to come to a close
I hope I've not trodden on anyone's toes
A good New Year to the price of gold
It keeps the nasty wolf from the fold
It shows that God is on our side
And with our ways is satisfied.
And so at last I'll say God bless
To Helen J and Helen S.
And so to Charmian and Ray
May tomorrow be a happy day.
For all that we do hold most dear
May this year be a Happy Year.

New Year's Eve, 1982
Unpublished

LIGHT VERSE

There was a sweet family, Thorrold . . .

There was a sweet family, Thorrold
Who never have snorted or quorrold,
That's all one can say
Except, by the way,
That they populate half of the worrold.

Untitled
Natal University College Magazine, 1923

Annual Report of the S.P.C.G., Year Ending October, 1923.

Dedication

A fine big fellow you are, my lad;
        two hundred if you are a pound,
                And you spend your days,
                    So rumour says,
                          Following grasshoppers round.

And you catch a poor little beggar, they say,
        you with your two hundred pound,
                And you drive a tack
                    Into its back,
                          The poor little beggar you've found.

And you put the poor little chap in a box, you
        with your two hundred pound,
                And to add to your fame
                  You give him a name,
                      Grashoppus Bushensis, or some
                              such fine sound.

And rumour is saying ('tis hard to believe), that
        you with your two hundred pound
                Shortly will be
                A blown M.Sc.
                    Whatever they say,
                    Be that as it may,
                      In the eyes of the
                        S.P.C.G. you're a
                              hound,
                    You and your two hundred pound.

Unsigned
Natal University College Magazine, 1923

156

Curlilocks . . .

"Curlilocks, Curlilocks, will you be mine?
      "Star of my lonely sky,
"Curlilocks, Curlilocks, angel divine,
      "Art thou for such as I?"

So I cried on the first-year night,
      And longed to see her again,
But alas and alack! in the broad daylight,
      Curlilocks was quite plain.

Unsigned and untitled
Natal University College Magazine, 1924

There's memory of laughter . . .

There's memory of laughter, memory
      Of sin, and shame that follows after,
if then you would remember me
      Remember the laughter.

Probably Ixopo, 1930
Unpublished and untitled

Night is dark . . .

Night is dark, leaving him unknowing
If day will dawn with the sun in the sky
Or grey clouds, coming and going.

He lies at peace, and the new turned sod
Is returned to its place: Is it sun in the sky?
Or clouds? Leave it to God.

Probably Ixopo, 1930
Unpublished and untitled

157

It's quite clear . . .

It's quite clear that your manners
Have gone into retreat.
You saw the lady standing,
And yet you took the seat.

Written in 1933
Unpublished and untitled

A knock there comes . . .

A knock there comes upon my door
    As loud as loud can be
A thought-policeman stands without
    And that's the end of me.

Undated
Unpublished and untitled

The New Physics

dedication:

MESHAM! EDDINGTON! JEANS! Noble alliance!
What art but yours deserves the name of Science?
Let huxley, bush, and animalculus
Pay homage to your Tensor Calculus!
To abiotic heights can bews or bayer
For all their chlorophyll dare to aspire?
Let ferguson and freud their dreams abjure
And seek where PHYSICS breathes an air more pure.
And jehu, who for bread gives men but stone,
Adjourn to chew a mesozoic bone.

158

Hail! SPLENDID THREE! Ineffable alliance!
Now for the lesser lights of your great Science!
mckinnell? — yes, we'll grant a bare admission
To keep your books, and fluke by intuition.
And coutts we'll find a few appropriate tasks,
To test live wires and clean out your flasks.
Admit as satellites beckett and kurruk
To do the sidelines of your MAJOR WURRUK.
And then no more — avaunt, inanities!
No place, no space, for your humanities.
Renounce all claim to Science, vain pretensions!
Go and decline with thanks petrie's declensions.
Go learn from hattersley of this and that war
Or hark to mary leiper lisp her patois.
Or humble-hearted, follow what does follow,
For Modern PHYSICS beats houdini hollow.

PHYSICS — (made easy)

Do you know modern PHYSICS? Well, listen hard to my
Pellucid exposition, for you really ought to try.
We'll want a standard ruler and a reputable clock . . .

    And we'd better have handy
    A case of brandy
    In case of shock.

Before we're very far advanced we're almost sure to find
We might as usefully have left the clock and rule behind.
For the clock immediately goes wrong — it may be fast or slow,
And the rule's immediately too long — or it may be short, you
    know.
For clocks and rules are useless in this higher PHYSICS game —
If you drink the case of brandy the results are just the same.
Now here we have an atom, but you can't look and see.
For if you did, the thing is not what it once used to be.
We first have small electrons that go unheard-of speeds.
And when they're rousened it's been reckoned
Two hundred thousand miles per second
Is all —

Yes do, poor fellow,
No — just a tot.
Don't take the lot,
There's more to follow.

These electrons have position, we know just where about.
Their speeds — of course, I've told you — yes, we can find
    them out.
But on my oath, they can't have both . . .

Yes, have a spot
But not the lot.
There's more to follow.

What did you say?
The world is going to pot?
Ha! Ha! I can assure you it's absolutely not.
But relatively, what? Ha! Ha! who knows
If it's the world to pot, or pot to world that goes.

All right — a dot
But not the lot.
There's more to follow.

Now this atomic world we know a lot about.
Is Mr Electron in? We'll look — that puts him out.
We put him out by looking, gave him a quantum.
What? you don't understand? there's reasons if you want 'em.
See EDDINGTON — Chapter three — ah yes! it's here —
It's like a sweepstake — well that's quite clear.
And what's the reason? that you'll never guess.
It's free-will, like our own, these things possess.

All right — a jot
But not the lot.
There's more to follow.

What's that? you're feeling worse?
Well I'll be clear and terse
And state our last resort.

160

(Where's JEANS? ah wait — it's Chapter eight)
— You see — the universe —
Is like — well — like a thought.

    Yes, have the lot
    For nobody can follow.

Nothing's absolutely nor absolutely not.
Ultimately therefore, no one knows what's what.
Something's doing something, somewhere, don't you see?
Everything's spontaneous, just like you and me.
I'm sorry you can't follow, but you really ought to try.
I'll spare you the important proof that men don't really die.
No one really knows the rules in this higher physics game,
But now you've had the BRANDY the results are just the same.

Natal University College Magazine, 1934

We Cogitate

We cogitate
Matters of State
Baring and Tait
With reckless daring
We are comparing
Tait and Baring
Will we be soon
Bearing with Baring?
Or tête à tête
With Tait?
I am past caring
Give me Tait or Baring
It's getting late
Give me Baring or Tait.
Probably 1946

Unpublished and untitled

Bus Passenger

You, bus passenger, with the fat buttocks,
Why are you smiling?
I have a mind to untrouser you,
And reach the bottom of the matter.

Probably Lane's Flat, 1949
Unpublished

162

The K.L.M.

The Dutch may be a stolid race
And noted for their phlegm,
But with what master touch and grace
They made the K.L.M.

Undated but probably written between November 1949 and January 1950
Unpublished

Confused . . .

Confused no doubt by words like 'choose'
You go on writing 'loose' for 'lose'
Soon you'll be writing 'ruse' for 'rues'
And 'Bruce' for 'bruise' and other blues.

If 'loose' is 'lose' then Heavens knows
What you will make of 'noose' and 'nose',
You'll squeeze our oranges for Jews,
And look for friends in old Hoose-Hoose.

How bright in church when pews are puce,
How shocked the ear when moos the moose,
How sad the sheep when fleas are fleece,
How glad the world if peas were peace.

Come Margaret dear, attention police,
Go down upon your bended niece,
And ask for even half the nous
Which Providence allows a louse.

Anerley; Paton to Margaret Snell, 13 February 1953
Unpublished and untitled

To Marion. 18.12.60

My apparently unwilling kookie
I took to unoverlooked nookie
I conquered her scruples
With dilated pupils
She said, You are clearly no rookie.

Unpublished

It has been said . . .

It has been said that Edgar's verse
Has year by year got worse and worse
Then why this year this sudden change,
A deeper depth, a stronger strength,
And oh alas a longer length
A wider-ranging kind of range?

Undated, but read at Paton's birthday, 11 January 1979
Unpublished and untitled

Ode to the New *Reality*

A Journal of Liberal and Radical Opinion

Dedicated to
Edgar Brookes —
Old champion
of the right
New champion of
the left.

Sometimes I was a glad lib
Sometimes I was a sad lib
No more I'll be a bad lib
For now I am a rad lib.

I never was a mad rad
I would have made a bad rad
Although I hate the glib rad
Myself am now a lib rad

Lib now takes its sabbatical
But I'll not be fanatical
I shall remain pragmatical
Though I am now a radical.

No more I'll lie and fiberal
Nor talk a lot of gibberal
Nor will I wait and quiberal
I now am a rad liberal.

I really now have had lib
Now that I am a rad lib
I pledge to the new REALITY
My firm and true feality.

Reality, 1973

165

POEMS FOR CHILDREN

Who Likes Me?

Who likes me?
Nobody.

Paton to Marigold Burns, 23 September 1948
Unpublished and untitled

I can see Kitty

I can see Kitty
Brighty can see Kitty
Mum can see Kitty
Dad can see Brighty
Brighty can see no parking
Kitty can see Jon.
Kitty and Brighty can see Jon and Mum.
Jon can see Brighty under the table.

Written in the late 1930s
Unpublished

Hal

Dear Hal, I only want to say
The rain is raining every day
No boys can run, no boys can play
Because the rain won't stay away.

Thence warm sun I never see.
Where do you think the sun can be?
The time is only half-past three
But there's no sun at all for me.

The rain must stop, it really must
Tomorrow will be fine, I trust,
To find another rhyme I'm bust
So shall end with this, non-plussed.

Paton to Aubrey Burns, 13 January 1950
Unpublished

LAST JOURNEY

RETURN

REFLECTIONS

Sonnet

I saw Them playing with Their bauble, Earth,
Death leering from His bony, fleshless face,
Plague in His foul, dank rags in His foul place,
And Mammon laughing in his hellish mirth.
I saw Them toss it, hurl it, to and fro,
I heard tombed crying and it rose and fell
Like nigh unutterable anguish of some hell
That dares not think if there is hope or no.
I saw Death reap rich harvests of the dead,
Plague cast His pestilence on sea and land,
And hellish Mammon urging on the game.
And while I watched Them, lo! a Fourth there came
And snatched Their bauble from each clutching hand,
Then loud as thunder, 'I have come,' He said.

Natal University College Magazine, 1924

(See Notes at the end for further references to the various poems)

Sterility

When I was young my songs I sang
I thought their like could never be,
Now I am old and know the worth
Of all the songs that are on earth
They seem such artless melody.

And now with ripe and mellow songs
That from the womb call me and call
I find I cannot sing at all.

Undated, but probably written in 1928
Unpublished

Evening

Peace on the meadowland,
Peace on the hill,
The voice of my Lord
'Peace, be still.'
Red of the sunset
Dies on the hill,
Lone in the furrow
Night doth till.

Natal University College Magazine, 1929

When the last sleep comes . . .

When the last sleep comes, lay me to rest
Among the green rolling hills I know,
Lay me to rest, command my soul to quiet,
And when I'm laid, and soul commanded, go.

And I will rise with joy and laughter
Sing with the grass larks in the sun and rain,
Fly with the wild wind thro' the boughs of heaven
And know no rest nor quietness again.

They will hear my laughter on the windy hills
And never know or dream that it is mine,
They will say the wind blows cold and wildly
And shrink round the fire when they hear it whine.

They will all forget me, forget my place of rest,
Forget that I was born, ever lived or ever died,
And I will laugh wildly, for what care I,
My friends are the spirits of the countryside.

And what if I should find there, one who yet weeps,
What will it help then to fly in wind and rain;
When the heart's great desire, now that I am dead,
(If one still weeps for me), is to be alive again.

Undated, but probably Ixopo 1929
Unpublished and untitled

Retreat! Retreat! . . .

Retreat! Retreat!
Sound it, trumpets, as the only call
To save our souls from the icy tomb,
Help the child go back to the friendly womb
For its dark is kinder than any light
And its closeness sweeter than any room.
Retreat! Retreat!
Sound it, trumpets, as the only call
To call man back from a ruthless life
To quiet and peace from the ugly strife.

Undated, but probably Ixopo 1930
Unpublished and untitled

173

The Incurable

Doctors and nurses day by day
Pass me with no new word to say
Except 'you're fine, you're looking fine'
But give no chance for me to say
A single word of mine.

I see my name is now removed
From the lists of the approved
To the private list of dead
I see they wait and all unmoved
For my death and bed.

The family visits true and steady
But young eyes wonder now already
They ask as ever, how's our friend
But not a word of my returning
They too accept the end.

I bide my time when I am chidden
And laugh to think of knowledge hidden.
For such as these I keep concealed
Knowledge that's come to me unbidden
I know I shall be healed.

I keep this secret from the prying
One night down the rows of dying
There'll come a doctor, and no soul
Shall see him reach the shining hand
That lifts and makes me whole.

I want to shout it in the night
And fill this living morgue with fright
With doctors, nurses, running, crying
Silence, silence, silence, silence
That's the rule for dying.

I laugh to think what will be said
When standing by my empty bed
They judge me with some angry name
Who left without due notice said
When the shining doctor came.

Undated, but could have been written when Paton had typhoid in 1934 or at Lane's Flat , 1949
Unpublished

Death

I have seen the ways of Death
Till I feel that I know him to face,
But things are the same tomorrow
And the sounds of the place.

He has walked in the homes that I knew
And called for a friend and a foe,
But the sun shines the same tomorrow
On hills that I know.

Yet I shall cry like a child
When He takes what is mine from me.
Though things are the same tomorrow
What help will it be?

Natal University College Magazine, 1932

Only the Child Is No More

The sea roars as ever it did
The great green walls travel landwards
Rearing up with magnificence
Their wind-blown manes.

His wonderment I recapture here
I remember his eyes shining
I remember his ears hearing
Unbelievable music.

I hear it now, but the high notes
Of excitement are gone
I hear now deeper
More sorrowful notes.

All is the same as ever it was
The river, the reed lagoon
The white birds, the rocks on the shore
Only the child is no more.

Anerley, 1948
Knocking on the Door, 1975

The world is changing too fast for me . . .

The world is changing too fast for me.
I remember the valley of the Umzimkulwana
When I was a boy, how it was my kingdom
Shared only with redwing sprews and the oribi
And the iguana crashing away startled
Through the undergrowth: but the undergrowth is gone
And the huts of the Indians stand nakedly
Where the oribi stood silent as stone
Under my eyes; and the kingdom of childhood,
The sacred inviolable places, the glades and the glories
Are desecrated by the alien encroachments
Of uncountable Indians, much more than I ever remember
When I was a boy.

Undated, but probably January 1949
Unpublished and untitled

1950-1984

The tributary widens, I sense an urgency in the water
The trees and the sky seem to say to me
Some greatness is imminent.
The stream quickens, it is aware of its destiny
And I am fearful and exalted,
For I shall see the great falls and the smoke that thunders
Of which I have heard since childhood.
Now I yield to the current, now I struggle against it
I am uplifted, I am cast down by this solemn journey.

Undated: written initially in response to Paton's visit to the Victoria Falls in 1950, he later rewrote it
in a way that compares the Victoria Falls to the Iguazu Falls in South America which he visited at the
end of 1984
Unpublished

ALTERNATIVE VERSIONS AND OTHER WORKINGS

I saw in a dream . . .

1. I saw in a dream a certain man who with his wife and his children lived in a well-favoured country, which was all that a man could desire. Everything there was perfect but for one thing, and that was a certain beast that lived there. And the thought came into the man's mind that one day the beast would turn and devour them all.

2. Therefore he built an enclosure, fencing it around with iron and wood. And he enticed the beast into it, and closed the gate on it. Then he gave all his mind to his labour.

3. And the beast went to and fro in the place where it was captive, and filled day and night with its roaring. It ceased not from roaring, nor from going to and fro in its captivity.

4. But the enclosure was stout and strong, so the man laughed at the roaring of the beast, and gave little other thought to it.

5. Sometimes the beast was full of fury, and broke its teeth on the iron and wood, and threw itself against the fence in its anger.

6. And the man's friends said to him, the beast was surely young, for it is growing bigger and stronger. Make the fence yet stronger, or build another round the first, against a day of disaster.

7. So he built a second fence round the first, stouter and stronger. And the beast saw the second fence, and in its fury threw itself against the first. And it broke down the first, and threw itself now against the second.

8. So the man's fear returned to him, and he built a third fence round the second, even stouter and stronger.

9. Because of his fear, he built night and day, so that the fields were not tilled, and the cattle not cared for. And his children went hungry, and complained to him of their hunger.

10. Then he was angered that they complained to him, and did not see that what he did was only for them. But he said to them, let me finish this third fence, then let us eat and drink and be merry, and live without fear in this country. So he built the third fence and finished it.

11. And the beast broke through the second fence, and threw itself in fury against the third which was exceedingly stout and strong. Nevertheless he built a fourth fence for the sake of their peace, stouter and stronger than them all.

12. Now he slept not, but laboured without end. And even when he slept, he would wake in fear, and go to the fence. And the beast went to and fro, and he went to and fro with it; when the beast turned, he turned; and when the beast slept, he slept; and when the beast woke from its sleep, he woke also, and went to and fro with the beast.

13. And the beast broke through the third fence, and the man set himself to build a fifth. He scoured the land for wood and for iron, and impoverished himself and his children, and heard no more the song of any bird, and rejoiced no more in the rain. For his only thought was the thought of the beast, and he had no thought for the pleasure and labour of a man.

14. And in my dream I cried out to him, brother, thou art in captivity. And he woke from his sleep, and stretched out his arms to me, and I saw the anguish of his eyes. And he would have answered me, but that the beast woke at my cry, and roared with anger, and went to and fro in its captivity. Therefore he rose, and went to and fro with the beast, and I could see that he said to himself, I must soon build another.

15. And I awoke, sweating and trembling, because of my dream of the man and the beast that he kept in captivity.

Unpublished and untitled
(See 'I Came to the Valley . . .' above)

I'll sting the conscience . . .

I'll sting the conscience of the world awake
With a fine pointed barb and a red-hot steel
To follow. I'll uncover the cold heart
And set her beating with a merciless message
And hear her cries unmoved when the awakened blood
Starts stinging the disused arteries
I'll dance like a madman on her chilled limbs
And set them up and working, I'll bring the heat of hell
To thaw out the frozen emotions
I'll have her spitting, laughing, crying

I'll burn the frigidity out of her
And make her fit for a hot soul to marry.

(first version)

I'll stab the conscience of the world awake
With seven fine-pointed barbs, and shafts
Of red-hot steel to follow, I'll uncover
Her frozen heart, and set it beating yet
With massage of brass gloves, steel rasped, pointed
With diamonds, and hear her cries unmoved
When the awakened blood goes thudding through
The disused arteries, like a blind swarm
Of angry wasps, I'll dance fanatic
On her chilled frame, and set it up and running
I'll thaw the iced emotions out with hell's
Own heat, I'll have her spitting, laughing, crying
I'll burn frigidity out of her limbs
And make her fit for a hot soul to marry.

(second version)

Unpublished and untitled
(See 'I'll Stab the Conscience of the World Awake' above)

The Incurable

I lie here and wait by myself
Day by day the doctors pass me,
The nurses, right past where I lie,
But not one has a new word for me.
But to say in passing, how is my friend
And go, waiting for no reply.

I lie here and wait by myself
I see that I am condemned
I see that the list of the dead
Have one name more. I see
That they wait only without speaking
For my death and my bed.

I lie here and wait by myself
My friends ask no more about my returning
Tho' they come ever faithful and steady.
They speak so no longer, the old
Look at me with pity, the young
With eyes that are elsewhere already.

I lie here and wait by myself
But I have knowledge that is hidden
Strong and burning, but I keep it concealed.
Knowledge strong beyond any doubting
Knowledge burning beyond any quenching
I know that I shall be healed.

I lie here and wait by myself
But I know Someone will come for me
When all are asleep, and never a soul
Shall see the Shining One come to me
All down between the rows of the dying
And lift me up and I shall be whole.

I lie here and wait by myself
I want to shout out my hope in the night.
But do not want them running over the floor
Saying to me, this is most disobedient,
As tho' no hope, no shrieking no crying
Could bring something new any more.

So I lie here and wait by myself
And picture their wrath. They will find
No bad enough name for me
And stand in amazement by my bed
To find my place no more tenanted
At the call of that One Who came for me.

Unpublished
(See 'The Incurable' above)

The tributary widens . . .

The tributary widens, I sense an urgency in this water
The trees and the sky seem to say to me, some greatness is imminent.
The stream quickens, it is aware of its destiny
And I am fearful and exalted, for I shall see the great river
I seem to have known of it always, tho' it was but dimly apprehended.
Sometimes I yield to the current, sometimes I struggle and exert
    myself
I thrash about in my fear, I am oppressed by this solemn journey
I move from side to side uncertainly, not yet convinced of this
    destination
I know if I am to leave . . .

Written 1950
Unpublished and untitled (See '1950-1984' above)

Necklace of Fire

I send you a present, my love, my love,
Though not of my own desire
The comrades say it's my duty, my love
This present of terrible beauty, my love
The necklace of fire.

They say I need not be present, my love
To stand at the funeral pyre
So long as you know that I sent it, my love,
The necklace of fire.

It is the children, my love, my love.
It is the children who now require
That I must send you this present, my love
The necklace of fire.

They say they must die for the cause, my love
But you say obey the laws, my love
So the children say you must die, my love
With the necklace of fire.

182

It is the children, my love, my love,
Oh how can I tell you, my love, my love?
It is our children, my husband, my love
It is our children who now require
That it's your wife who must end your life
With the necklace of fire.

It will be tomorrow, my love, my love
It is tomorrow that the comrades require
And if I say that I cannot agree
Then the comrades may also order for me
The necklace of fire.

(first version)

I send you a present, my love, my love,
Though not of my own desire,
I send you a present my dearest love,
I send you a necklace of fire.

I told them I would not send it, my love
A present so dire.
The children laughed in my face, my love
I never thought to see such a day
They said, if you dare to disobey
What the comrades require,
Then you too will get the necklace of fire.

What has become of the children, my love
The children, our children, my husband, my love?
They say they will die for the cause
But you teach them to obey the laws,
Therefore for you the comrades require
The necklace of fire.

They say you will wear it tomorrow, my love
I think with unspeakable sorrow, my love
For what shall I do with the rest of my life
Who now am no longer mother or wife.

(second version)

Unpublished
(See 'Necklace of Fire' above)

NOTES

FIRST JOURNEY: BEGINNINGS

EARLY IMPRESSIONS

To a Picture: *Natal University College Magazine,* 1, November 1920, p.8. Paton identified this poem (and others like it in which he uses a pseudonym) as his in his copy of the *NUC Magazine.*

The Sea: *Natal University College Magazine,* 3, May 1921, pp.48-9. Although it is signed L.T. it is listed in the contents page as that of A.P.

Sonnet — To Sleep: *Natal University College Magazine,* 7, 1922, p.29.

Song of the Northward-Bound: *Natal University College Magazine,* 7, 1922, pp.34-5. It seems that Paton was attracted to this (anapestic) rhythm in a poem 'The North-Bound Mail' (J.L. Lawn), which was published in *The Eisteddfod Poetry Book* (1921), pp.68-9. (Paton's poem 'You and I' was also published in this collection.) The similarity between these two poems can be seen in the first stanza of Lawn's poem:

> List to the song of the north-bound mail,
> Freighted with hopes and fears,
> Spurning the touch of the gleaming rail,
> Heedless of smiles and tears,
> Joyously garnering vale and hill,
> Flashing o'er river and babbling rill,
> Servant of Man, but triumphant still,
> Power personified.

"Colenso plain" refers to the expansive grasslands outside the town of Colenso in KwaZulu/Natal.

COLLEGE POEMS

Old Walls . . . : *Maritzburg College Magazine,* November 1934. It also appears in Paton's autobiography *Towards the Mountain* (p.35) and in Anne Paton's story of her life with Alan Paton, *Some Sort of a Job* (p.258).

School: Maritzburg College was founded in 1863. It is a Government School (which means that it is not privately owned) and has boarding facilities.

Trilemma: *Natal University College Magazine,* 26, 1932, p.34, and in *Knocking on the Door,* 1975, p.12.

Memories 1919-1924: *Natal University College Magazine*, 29, 1929, pp.13-14.
"N.U.C.": Natal University College;
"Adolf": Adolf Bayer, a friend and University colleague of Paton's, who
later became Professor of Botany at the University of Natal;
"Freddie": is probably Frank Bush, zoologist and educator and Vice-
Principal of the University of Natal (Pietermaritzburg);
"Nuttall . . . D.H.S.": Neville Nuttall was a university friend, walking
companion and literary ally of Paton's;
Durban High School, like Maritzburg College, is an old, well-established
school, which Nuttall attended and where he later taught;
"Richardson . . . Rhodes": refers to Matthew Richardson who studied
History and Latin at N.U.C., and who won the Rhodes Scholarship in
1929;
"Old Mooney" refers to Jack Mooney who studied Law at N.U.C. and
practised as an attorney in Pietermaritzburg, and
"Dr Bronstein" was a doctor of medicine and dentistry who qualified in
both professions and who practised as a dentist in Pietermaritzburg.

POEMS OF SETTLEMENT AND HISTORY

Ladysmith: *Natal University College Magazine*, 4, November 1921, pp.10-11.
Ladysmith is a town in the interior of KwaZulu/Natal. The "Battlefields"
is a reference to either the siege of Ladysmith or the battle of Spioen
Kop during the South African War (1899-1902).

The grass-larks' call . . . : "Kununata" is near High Flats on the road between
Ixopo and Park Rynie, KwaZulu/Natal. There are also references here
to a British soldier's grave and the South African War.

Maritzburg in February: *Natal University College Magazine*, 26, 1932, p.25.

The farmers know . . . : "Lodesborough" (or "Ladesborough") may be a
colloquial name for a village or farm in KwaZulu/Natal.

SECOND JOURNEY: AWAKENING

POEMS OF DESIRE AND REDEMPTION

You and I: *The Eisteddfod Poetry Book*, December 1921, pp.37-8. Paton
entered it for the 1921 Eisteddfod competition.

Sonnet I ("Far out the waves are calling, Marguerite"): *Natal University
College Magazine*, 6, 1922, pp.19-21.

186

To —: *Natal University College Magazine*, 9, 1923, pp.88-9. It also appears in a letter from Paton to R.O. Pearse, 21 January 1922. Possibly written (under the influence of De la Mare) at the beginning of 1922, if not at the end of 1921.

Gemellia: *Natal University College Magazine*, 10, 1924, p.26. This poem was probably written in the second half of 1923, if not earlier. It first appears in a letter to Pearse, 5 December 1923. Paton also says in this letter, using 'Gemellia' as an example, that: "The modern spirit, when not in Bolshevik revolution, produces amazing stuff, stuff coming into being offering no explanation of its birth, shrouded in mystery (not obscurity, Pearse)."

Sister Street: *Natal University College Magazine*, 12, 1925, p.45. "Sister Street" could be an orientalist allusion to what was reputed to be a place of excess and pleasure in Cairo.

The Prostitute: The phrase "sister of the street" could be an allusion to the poem 'Sister Street' above.

Scottsville, 1931: *Natal University College Magazine*, 24, 1931, p.12. Scottsville is a suburb of Pietermaritzburg.

Poor Whites: *Natal University College Magazine*, 24, 1931, p.22. The term "poor whites" was used to describe impoverished (mainly Afrikaans-speaking) farmers who had moved to the cities following the 1929 economic depression;
"veldskoen": traditional Afrikaner shoes.

The Prodigals: *Natal University College Magazine*, 28, May 1933, p.26.

Sanna: *Knocking on the Door*, 1975, p.111. A corrected version was sent to Mary Benson on 3 April 1949.

The Prison House: Published in *Instrument of Thy Peace*, 1968 , pp.127-28, and in *Knocking on the Door*, 1975, pp.29-30. According to Paton's 1949 diary it was written at the end of a Toc H Conference which he attended in 1949. In the original manuscript the last line has various alternatives: "The chains that were like no other that ever were known to me," or, "The chains that now are become like brothers/lovers to me."

Sonnet — To Sleep I: "for relief" has the alternative "grateful" in a letter to Aubrey Burns, 26 December 1951.

Sonnet — To Sleep II: "caressing fingers" could also read "reposeful fingers" as in the letter above.

The blood poured . . . : This poem was found among the papers of Aubrey and Marigold Burns. It is accompanied by one or two poems by Aubrey

Burns himself. It was probably written when Burns went to stay with Paton at Lane's Flat in January 1950. Although in Paton's handwriting — with no corrections — it is possible that Paton and Burns co-operated in its composition, but we cannot be sure of its origins. It also appears alongside a humorous poem by Paton, 'To a Bus Passenger' (see below).

This love is warm . . . : This poem was found in the margins of Paton's 1950 diary. Although we cannot be certain of the authorship, it is written in Paton's handwriting (and includes corrections). It was probably written in New York, and appears in his diary on the day after his visit to Mrs Roosevelt in her capacity as a Member of the Human Rights Commission of the United Nations. He had presumably approached her — as he does again in 1955 — in order to draw her attention to the racial policies of the National Party Government. Line 5 is difficult to decipher and the word "clean" could read "clear" or something similar.

To a Small Boy Who Died at Diepkloof Reformatory: *Knocking on the Door*, 1975, pp.68-9. Dorrie Paton sent a number of poems to Paton (which he had written at Anerley) while he was staying at Lane's Flat in December 1949. One of the poems, 'The House of the World is Falling' — which Paton records as "promising" — is probably the original title of this poem. It seems that it was revised a number of times after it was first written in March 1949.

TRANSLATIONS AND TRANSITIONS

Sonnet II ("Give me my sword . . ."): *Natal University College Magazine*, 6, 1922, p.21.

Old Til: *Natal University College Magazine*, 9, October 1923, p.7, and in *Knocking on the Door*, 1975, pp.2-3.

Felip': *Natal University College Magazine*, 10, June 1924, pp.38-41.

The Future: *Natal University College Magazine*, 28, May 1933, p.28.

The Bull-Frog: *Natal University College Magazine*, 28, May 1933, p.30. Paton had been working at the time on what he later termed "novels of 'country life'", which were never published. In the second half of 1932 he had written a play, *Louis Botha*, which after a number of rewritings was finally rejected by the Repertory Play-Reading Society in 1935. The issue of having his work published could have been a pressing concern for Paton in the early 1930s.

Translation: *Natal University College Magazine: Commemoration Number, 1909-1934*, October 1934, p.47, and in *Knocking on the Door*, 1975, p.14.

Lied van die Verworpenes [Song of the Outcasts]: *Contact*, July 1957. There exist various versions and titles to this poem. One, 'Engelse Liedjie' [English Song], was sent to J.H. Hofmeyr on 22 December 1938. Paton wrote this poem two days after attending the 1938 Eeufees Celebrations — the Centenary Celebrations of the Great Trek — where he discovered the exclusive nature of Afrikaner nationalism and its racial antagonism (Paton to Hofmeyr, 22 December 1938).

SONGS OF DISCOVERY AND AFFIRMATION

Reverie: It is unclear when this poem was written. The only version is this revised one which appears in a letter to Pearse, 10 June 1923; "veldt" is a variation of the spelling of "veld" (grassland).

House of Dreams: *Natal University College Magazine*, 8, December 1923, p.15. Paton wrote an essay in the same magazine, 'A Happy Evening', and signed it Kidney Slark. K.S. could stand for Sidney Clark; "kloof" is an Afrikaans word for a gully or ravine.

Song: *Natal University College Magazine*, 12, 1925, pp.45-6. This poem was written at Centocow, a black mission school near Braecroft in KwaZulu/Natal, where Paton had spent the end of 1923 invigilating examinations. He makes a number of observations, both literary and political, regarding this experience in a letter to Pearse, 5 December 1923. One is that though he is drawn to what he calls "Native Work", he feels ambivalent about its significance for him in the future. Another is that he regards what he terms the "modernist" "joy in realism" as a "dangerous taste." He says that "realistic art is as good as any other art, but the tendency is to be so overpowered by realism that one forgets to demand the art." Moreover, he says that "the love idyll and the gaunt tragedy are as essential to literature as are the green hills and the vast desert to nature." It was probably written between 3 and 9 December 1923; "Hlabeni": There is a place called Hlabeni near Bulwer in KwaZulu/Natal, but it could also be on the south coast of KwaZulu/Natal.

Tugela, Tugela, sweep on . . . . : In a letter to Pearse at the beginning of 1925, Paton says that this poem is "my idea of the Thorns" — which is an area between Pietermaritzburg and Ladysmith to which Paton, Pearse and Cyril Armitage regularly hiked. "Tugela" is a river which formed the border between what was originally Natal and Zululand; "krantz" is an Afrikaans word for a rocky cliff; "aasvogels": Afrikaans for vultures.

Carton: Sydney Carton appears in Dickens' A *Tale of Two Cities*. The idea of Carton redeeming himself through self-sacrifice — he is executed in the place of the French aristocrat, Charles Darnay — could have had some significance for Paton at the time. The themes of moral reform and self-sacrifice are prominent in Paton's work. Neville Nuttall writes in his 1923 diary that Paton "is remarkably original — I imagine he has a spark of genius — he has a rather fine scheme of dramatising the (sic) *Tale of Two Cities.*" Jolyon Nuttall kindly provided this information for us.

Sonnet ("There's no way carved . . ."): *Natal University College Magazine: Commemoration Number, 1909-1934,* October 1934, p.52, and in *Knocking on the Door,* 1975, p.13. It was written near the end of a three month period on the south coast holiday resort of Park Rynie, where Paton spent recuperating from typhoid fever.

From where the sun pours . . . : This poem was written in Sweden in 1946. *Cry, the Beloved Country* was begun a week later in Trondheim, Norway.

Singer of Childhood: Although Paton began writing this poem after 'To Walt Whitman' (below), these two poems seem to overlap in many ways. There is a German translation of this poem called 'Igudugudu, Kindheitssänger' which forms part of the original manuscript, and with a note by Paton to the effect that the Igudugudu is a bird - "Burchell's Coucal" (The Rainbird).

In the Umtwalumi Valley: *Knocking on the Door,* 1975, p.70. According to Paton's 1949 diary it could have been written in March 1949, as he had just returned to Anerley from Cape Town, via High Flats and Ixopo.

The mist comes down . . . : "titihoya" is a bird of the plover species.

I came to a valley . . . : Another version of this poem 'I Saw in a Dream...' appears in *Alternative Versions and Workings* above.

I Have Approached: *Contrast,* December 1961, and in *Knocking on the Door,* 1975, p.74. It first appears in a talk 'Why I Write', given in New York on 7 November 1949 (*Knocking on the Door* pp.75-83).

To Walt Whitman: *Knocking on the Door,* 1975, pp.62-3. Original referred to as 'In Trondheim'. In the final version there is a significant shift from the first person narrative to the third.

THIRD JOURNEY: POEMS OF CONSCIENCE

POLITICS AND PHILANTHROPY

I Take This Africa: Appears in Paton's diary of 1950 (22 January 1950) along with a map of his journey to various countries in Africa. He left Lane's

Flat on 21 January, although it seems unlikely that he wrote the poem in America. It is possible that the poem was written during July 1950.

We Mean Nothing Evil Towards You: *Knocking on the Door*, 1975, pp.114-15. Paton appears to refer to this poem in his 1949 diary as 'Cohabit No Longer with Fear'.

Could You Not Write Otherwise?: *Knocking on the Door*, 1975, pp.82-3. It first appears in 'Why I Write' on 7 November 1949 (*Knocking on the Door* pp.75-83). Paton seems to mention this poem in his 1949 diary (22 December) when he writes: "On revising 'Why do I Write Otherwise' thought it quite good."

The Laughing Girls: *Knocking on the Door*, 1975, p.98.

The Discardment: *Knocking on the Door*, 1975, p.72. An earlier version differs slightly in that line 10 reads "To strangers passing by", and three lines have been taken out in the second stanza:
"So for nothing is made
Compensation for a home and children
And an emasculated life
So for nothing . . ."

Dancing Boy: *Knocking on the Door*, 1975, pp.65-6. This final version was written on 18 June 1974. Paton's 1949 diary has a variation on the last two lines of the first verse:
"And when you had finished dancing
The white people threw money to you."

Indian Woman: *Knocking on the Door*, 1975, p.100. A copy was sent to Mary Benson on 15 November 1948.

The Stock Exchange: *Knocking on the Door*, 1975, p.73. It appears initially in a talk Paton gave in New York on 7 November 1949. Of the poem he says, "It is an interesting fact that some of my friends find this piece, which was written with a teasing rather than an earnest intention, bitter and painful." ('Why I Write', *Knocking on the Door*, p.79).

Durban: *Knocking on the Door*, 1975, p.81. First appears in 'Why I Write' on 7 November 1949.

To a Person Who Fled to Rhodesia: Published in the Liberal pamphlet *Contact*, 1(12), 12 July 1958. Rhodesia, now Zimbabwe, is the former colony of Britain.

I ask you, Indian people . . . : Appears in Paton's 1949 diary. There were extensive riots in and around Durban on 13 January, reaching as far as Anerley. In a week of racial conflict, sparked off by an assault on a Zulu youth by an Indian shopowner, 142 people died. This poem is also one of

191

the five poems forwarded to Paton by Dorrie Paton while he was staying at Lane's Flat in 1949. The poem, though untitled, is referred to by Paton as 'Tell me, Indians'. He also says in this diary that this poem is "well worth working on". There is some difficulty deciphering Paton's handwriting in the second last line, and it could read: "I shall make them sound like any voice of guns" or " . . . angry voice of guns".

Anxiety Song of an Englishman: *Knocking on the Door*, 1975, p.112.

To a Black Man Who Lost a Child Thro' Starvation: Appears in Paton's Lane's Flat diary as 'Black Man do not Weep or be Sorrowful' for which he adds the comment, "not poetry";
"predicants": the Afrikaans word for minister of religion;
". . . of Parktown and Musgrave Road and Rondebosch/ And Vrededorp and Greyville and Salt River" refers to different South African suburbs which are characterised by their wealth or poverty. Parktown is an affluent suburb in Johannesburg, whereas Vrededorp is, or was, a working-class area. In Durban, Musgrave Road is an affluent area, while Greyville is not. The same comparison can be made between Rondebosch and Salt River in Cape Town;
"Nationalists and United Party" refers to the two major white political parties at the time;
"the Carlton", "Grand National", the "Mount Nelson", "the Royal and the Hilton" are select hotels in Johannesburg , Cape Town and Durban;
"Rand Club and Country Clubs" are elite clubs in Johannesburg;
"Metro, the Playhouse, and the Alhambra" are theatres in Johannesburg, Durban and Cape Town, respectively.

Black Woman Teacher: *Knocking on the Door*, 1975, p.100. The poem was sent to Mary Benson on 14 September 1949. It was probably written at the same time, or just after, 'Could You Not Write Otherwise?' (17 August 1949) as it appears as part of the same manuscript. Paton says in *Towards the Mountain* that he wrote the poem "as a gift for Mrs Takalani" (p.251), a teacher in the Bavenda area (in the northern parts of South Africa) and friend of Edith Rheinallt-Jones.

Samuel: *Knocking on the Door*, 1975, p.71. Written after Paton's return from a tour of the Lake Districts in September 1949, according to his 1949 diary.

The Monument: The Voortrekker Monument, commemorating both the "Great Trek" and the "Day of the Vow" (the Afrikaner victory over the Zulu people at "Blood River"), was opened on 16 December 1949.

I'll stab the conscience . . . : is one of the psalm-like poems that Paton wrote at Lane's Flat. Two earlier versions appear in *Alternative Versions and Workings* above.

192

I am the Law . . . : The manuscript indicates that this poem was written on 25 and 26 February 1970; "homeland": racially segregated areas; "independence" has the word "freedom" written in as an alternative on the manuscript.

Death of a Priest: *Knocking on the Door*, 1975, p.227. This poem is addressed to Jimmy Kruger (1917-1987), who was the Minister of Justice.

Caprivi Lament: *Sunday Tribune*, Durban, 6 May 1973, and in *Knocking on the Door*, 1975, pp.260-61; "Springs", "Standerton" and "Lichtenburg" are towns close to Johannesburg; "Bloemfontein" is a provincial capital, and the legislative centre of South Africa.

Necklace of Fire: Paton wrote two subsequent versions of this poem (see *Alternative Versions and Workings* above). The manuscript contains different titles such as, 'A Present of Fire', 'The Comrades Require'. This is probably the last poem that he wrote.

PRAISES AND ELEGIES

On the Death of J.H. Hofmeyr: *The Forum*, 26 February 1949, and *Knocking on the Door*, 1975, p.67. Jan Hofmeyr (1894-1948) was a political leader and a friend of Paton's. As an enlightened political and administrative figure he represented a broad, inclusive South Africanism which involved, for people like Paton, the reconciliation of English and Afrikaans speaking people, and which could be extended to the unification of black and white people. Hofmeyr died suddenly at the end of 1948, which meant that the person destined to replace Smuts was lost to the liberal political movement. *Cry, the Beloved Country* is dedicated in part to Hofmeyr. Paton later wrote the story of Hofmeyr's life, *Hofmeyr*. There is some confusion around when this poem was written. Notes to the poem appear at the beginning of Paton's 1949 diary, but the manuscript suggests that the poem was written the day after Hofmeyr's death.
"great batsman": Although not a gifted sportsman, Hofmeyr was an enthusiastic cricketer. (*Towards the Mountain*, p.136)

To Edgar Brookes: Brookes (1897-1987) was a friend and political ally of Paton's. He was Principal of Adam's College (1933-1945) and President of the South African Institute for Race Relations. After the National Party victory at the end of 1948 — and with the death of J.H. Hofemeyr — Brookes became one of the few liberal voices left with political influence. A position that became more and more embattled as he found himself under pressure to resign from the Native Affairs Commission in 1949. He also served as a Senator on the Natives Representative Council.

Praise Song For Luthuli: Chief Albert Luthuli (1898-1967), President of the African National Congress, was banned and restricted to Groutville in 1959. Luthuli was presented with an ultimatum in October 1952 of either resigning from the ANC or giving up his Chieftainship. After refusing to do either he was stripped of his Chieftainship on 12 November 1952. In 1961 he was awarded the Noble Peace Prize. Like Hofmeyr, Luthuli represented for Paton a figure under whom national reconciliation could take place. This poem also appears in Mary Benson's *Chief Lutuli of South Africa*, 1963. Edward Callan, who has written extensively on Paton, wrote a biographical piece on Luthuli in 1960 (*Albert John Luthuli and the South African Race Conflict*) from which we have drawn (it was also submitted, among other documents, in support of Luthuli's nomination to the Nobel committee in Britain). "Groutville" is on the Umvoti River near Stanger in KwaZulu/Natal.

Flowers for the Departed: Written on the occasion of the killing of four students by the National Guard in a Vietnam anti-war protest at Kent State University (Ohio), May 1970. Read by Paton at Rhodes University in 1970. It was also broadcast in a programme put together by Edward Callan and Jonathan Paton "The Art and Life of Alan Paton", on 10 June 1970. It was subsequently published in the *New York Times*, May 1971. An American composer, Daniel Jahn, put it to music, and it was read into the Congressional Record by Congressman Ogden R. Reid.

SONGS FROM THE MUSICAL MKHUMBANE

The opening of the play was delayed after a call by Luthuli for a National Day of Mourning following the Sharpeville killings on 21 March. Set in Cato Manor — which became, like District Six and Sophiatown, a symbol of resistance to the policy of forced removals — the play opened on 29 March 1960. Paton wrote the lyrics for the songs which were put to music by Todd Matshikiza.

Opening Chorus: "Mkhumbane", which also appears as "Emkhumbane" in the manuscript, refers to Cato Manor and means "village in a gully".

Children's Song: Sung by children, it is a dialogue between a girl and a boy.

Tsotsi Song: "Tsotsi" seems originally to have referred to an urban person (male) who dressed in a particularly urbane way. It later came to be associated with someone who was anti-social.

194

Who Will You Marry?: A dialogue between young men and women or between "Tsotsis" and "Shop-girls".

Young Love: A note from Paton to Todd Matshikiza reads: "Not a sentimental, but rather a fresh sweet song. The note is given by line 20, shall we say? Don't hesitate to make minor alterations. Line 5 for example could just as well read 'Though you be near or far'".

Song (Rachel's Lament): The version in the original manuscript differs from this one in certain respects. The title, for example, is simply "Rachel's Song". The second line reads: "Why did you come to show to me", and line 5 has "waken" in place of "wake".

Bantustan: "Kwa Mashu" (Place of Marshall) is named after Marshall Campbell and is in KwaZulu/Natal.

FOURTH JOURNEY: SPIRITUAL EXERCISES

MEDITATIONS

Faith: *Natal University College Magazine*, 26, 1932, p.30, and *Knocking on the Door*, 1975, pp.10-11.

Meditation for a Young Boy Confirmed: Published in *The Christian Century*, 13 October 1954, pp.1237-9, and as an SPCK booklet, London 1959, and in *Knocking on the Door*, 1975, pp.86-93. The poem was started on 3 January 1950, and Paton was still working on it two days later: "Did nothing except fiddle with poem on J.[onathan]'s confirmation" (5 January 1950). Paton's son, Jonathan, was confirmed on 26 November 1949.

PSALMS AND DEVOTIONAL VERSE

No Place For Adoration: *Knocking on the Door*, 1975, p.84. According to Paton's diary, this is the first poem that he wrote while staying at Lane's Flat. He was also writing a novel at the time which dealt with Christ appearing in Johannesburg, to which the poem alludes; "Eloff Street" is the main street in Johannesburg.

My Lord has a great attraction . . . : Paton's Lane's Flat diary refers to this poem as Psalm 7. It is also appears in *Towards the Mountain* pp.291-92, and was initially published in the *South African Outlook*, 1 October 1953 p.148, as 'A Psalm';
"Alcatraz" refers to the well-known prison in the U.S.A.. Paton visited it on his penal tour in 1946/47, and described it as one of two

"unforgettable experiences" of the "ultimate conflict between man and society" (*Towards the Mountain* p.289). It was closed in 1963.

What is this sound . . . : It seems likely that this is one of the psalms written at Lane's Flat, which was thought to have been lost. It could be the psalm which Paton's diary refers to as 'My Lord Hearken to the Cries', Psalm 8, which was written on 13 December 1949.

A Psalm of the Forest: Published as 'A Psalm' in *South African Outlook*, 1 July 1953, p.110, and in *Knocking on the Door*, 1975, p.85, as 'A Psalm of the Forest'. Also referred to as 'A Modern Psalm', 'My Lord in the Forest', and in Paton's diary as 'Lord in the Forest,' Psalm 10; A variation on the last line includes: ". . . an exaltation, a glory".

Heavy with secret knowledge . . . : Although written in an exercise book containing poems from 1929, the handwriting seems to belong to the later work of Paton. It is possible that this poem is Psalm 10, 'Man's Knowledge', written at Lane's Flat in December 1949; "San Luis Rey" is a reference to the celebrated novel (1927) and film (1944) *The Bridge of the San Luis Rey*, by Thornton Wilder. The story revolves around the death of five travellers who die when a bridge collapses in Peru. The story is told by a Franciscan monk, Brother Juniper, who witnesses the accident in 1714. The central question is whether the accident is God's plan or not. Brother Juniper's book is burned by the Church elders at the end for being heretical.

For the earth is corrupted . . . : There is no indication in Paton's diary as to when exactly this psalm was written, although it probably belongs to those written at Lane's Flat at the end of 1949.

PRAYERS

O Lord give me that grace . . . : A prayer found in Paton's 1953 diary. It is difficult to know whether this is Paton's own prayer (there is one correction) or whether he has transcribed it from some other source; "J.C.": Jesus Christ.

Prayer: Written for John Patterson and published in the *Kent Quarterly*, Fall 1989.

A Daily Prayer For One's Work: This prayer was written in the back of a booklet called *Prayers We Have in Common - Agreed Liturgical Texts proposed by The International Consultation on English Texts*, and was found after Paton's death.

196

FIFTH JOURNEY: INDULGENCES

HUMOUR AND SATIRE

"No Responsibility Accepted" . . . Ed.: *Natal University College Magazine*, 20, 1929, p.97.

The Hermit: *Natal University College Magazine*, 24, May 1931, p.37. Published in *Knocking on the Door*, 1975 (pp.8-9) and in *Natal University College Magazine* as 'The Hermit', although the title on the manuscript is 'Retreat! Retreat!'.

My Sense of Humour: *Knocking on the Door*, 1975, p.124, but incorrectly dated.

The Chief: Anerley, 18 November 1948. Paton had written "reject" on the manuscript. The image here seems close to Paton's treatment of the inept chief in *Cry, the Beloved Country*.

The Joke: *Knocking on the Door*, 1975, p.113. One of the early titles of this poem was probably 'Cocktail Party'. Paton says that he attended a "show" at 8.00 p.m. in New York on 11 November — the opening of Anderson's musical adaptation of *Cry, the Beloved Country*, called *Lost in the Stars* — after which he wrote this poem. According to Peter Alexander (*Alan Paton*), "Someone made a joke about the tiny number of whites of liberal convictions" (p.276) at a Liberal Party meeting in Johannesburg. Paton's diary also suggests an alternative title to the poem as 'Man behind Bars'. A copy of the poem was also sent to Leslie Rubin on 13 January 1975. In the letter Paton says that he had just had his 75th birthday at which he read poems "from the days when I was resisting the LP [Liberal Party] and after I joined it".

Once in the Tavern . . . : After the publication of *Too Late the Phalarope*, there were a number of queries about where the phalarope was to be found. The novel is set in the Ermelo district of Gauteng (Transvaal). Jolyon Nuttall drew our attention to this poem (and its context) and supplied a handwritten copy of it.

My Great Discovery: *Africa South*, 1(3), April-June 1957. Also published in *Best Articles and Stories*, August-September 1958, and in *Knocking on the Door*, 1975, pp.118-21.

Dr Verwoerd my boss . . . : Written after Paton "had unexpectedly got a small writer's grant from the government" (Peter Alexander, *Alan Paton*, 1994, p.279).

INFORMAL WRITINGS

OCCASIONAL VERSE

Hail to the Chief: Gatsha Buthelezi: Inkatha leader and, at present, Minister of Home Affairs, who was a guest at Paton's birthday celebrations on a number of occasions;
"Brookes . . . Edgar on his doctorate": Edgar Brookes, who had just received an Honorary Doctorate from the University of Natal;
"imbongo": Imbongi or praise singer;
"northern fief": KwaZulu;
"Botha's Hill": Paton's home in KwaZulu/Natal;
"Hurley": Catholic Archbishop Denis Hurley of Durban — a friend and admirer of Paton's;
"Irene": Buthelezi's wife.

Prologue: Peter Stayt, an old friend of Paton's, lives in Underberg (KwaZulu/Natal) and is the widow of the blind anthropologist Hugh Stayt.

For Ray Swart's Fiftieth Birthday: Ray Swart was a member of parliament and leader of the Progressive Federal Party.

New Year's Eve 1982 at the Swarts': Ray Swart (see above);
"PFP": Progressive Federal Party;
"P.W": P.W. Botha, former State President and leader of the National Party;
"dis darem erg/ die groet bewoners van die Waterberg": Translated reads: "this is ominous/ the inhabitants of the Waterberg";
"Jaap Marais . . . old Vause": Marais was leader of Herstigte Nasionale Party and Vause Raw the leader of New Republic Party, both of whom lost support in the previous election;
"Rajbansi": Leader of the House of Delegates, which was formed to allow the Indian community to fit into the National Parties policy of "own affairs" and its tricameral parliamentary system;
"Gatsha": Gatsha Buthelezi (see above);
"Matanzimas": Kaiser Matanzima was the leader of the homeland of the Transkei. The reference is to the internecine conflict between various factions of the Matanzima clan;
"Mangope and Bophuthatswana": Lucas Mangope was the homeland leader of Bophuthatswana;
"Sol and the Sun Hotels": With the support of Mangope, Sol Kerzner and Sun Hotels opened up an entertainment centre (Sun City) in Bophuthatswana, which included the first legal casino. Various artists and entertainers were invited to perform there, and the Gary Player Golf Course was established with the co-operation of Player;
"SABC": South African Broadcasting Corporation which had the reputation of being the mouth piece of the National Party and its policies;

"Kim Shippey": Sports commentator for SABC at the time;
"Yarwell Nofine": Idiomatic expression: "Yes well, No fine";
"Artes": the SABC annual awards for entertainment;
"Sybil Hotz": Mayor of Durban;
"Boesak . . . NGK": Reverend Alan Boesak, United Democratic Front
(UDF) activist and member of the ANC. The National Intelligence,
after spying on him, made public an extra-marital affair he was having.
He was a Moderator of the Nederduitse Gereformeerde Sengingkerk,
which broke away from the Nederduitse Gereformeerde Kerk (NGK);
"Helen J and Helen S": Helen Joseph (1905-1995) and Helen Suzman,
both opponents in different ways of National Party policies. Helen
Joseph was banned and restricted for many years, whereas Helen
Suzman was the lone voice of opposition in Government.

LIGHT VERSE

There was a sweet family, Thorrold . . . : *Natal University College Magazine*,
6, 1922, p.27. Unsigned.

Annual Report of the S.P.C.G., Year Ending October, 1923: *Natal
University College Magazine*, 9, October 1923, p.51. S.P.C.G.: Special
Prevention of Cruelty to Grasshoppers. Frank Bush (biographical details:
'Memories 1919-1924', above) was researching grasshoppers in
Pietermaritzburg at the time.

Curlilocks . . . : *Natal University College Magazine*, 10, June 1924, p.18.

The New Physics: *Natal University College Magazine: Commemoration
Number, 1909-1934*, October 1934, pp.37-39. Original title, 'Higher
Physics';
"MESHAM! EDDINGTON! JEANS": Paul Mesham, Lecturer in
Physics, Natal University College. Sir Athur Eddington and Sir James
Jeans were both physicists and astronomers;
"ferguson": Professor Ferguson of Education, Natal University College;
"petrie's declensions": Alexander Petrie, professor of Classics at the
Natal University College.

A knock there comes. . . : Could have been written at the same time as 'The
Monument'.

We Cogitate: This typed poem was found in Paton's 1946 diary, which he
kept whilst travelling around Europe and North America (at the time
when he wrote *Cry, the Beloved Country*);
"Baring and Tait": Financial institutions in London.

The K.L.M.: Paton flew to the U.S. (and back) on K.L.M. when he went to
stay at Lane's Flat at the end of 1949 and the beginning of 1950.

Bus Passenger: Found among Aubrey Burns' papers.

Confused . . . : A letter from Margaret Snell to the Archivist at the Alan Paton Centre, 10 March 1991.

It has been said . . . : "Old champion of the right" is a reference to Edgar Brookes' initial support for J.B. Hertzog in the 1924 election and the policies of territorial segregation which he had argued for in his book, *The History of Native Policy in South Africa* (1924), and which he later recanted.

Ode to the New Reality: Written for *Reality*, 4, 6 January 1973. The poem arose in response to the maintenance of the word "Radical" in the subtitle of the journal, *Reality*, which Paton had opposed.

To Marion 18.12.60: Found in Paton's copy of the *Shorter Oxford Dictionary* after his death — thirty-five years after it was written.

It's quite clear . . . : Leif Egeland stood against a Mrs Benson in a parliamentary election in May 1933, which he won. Paton sent him this poem shortly after his victory. Quoted in Leif Egeland *Bridges of Understanding*, p.77.

POEMS FOR CHILDREN

Who Likes Me?: Paton says in this letter to Marigold Burns: "I send you one poem. I wrote it when I was six, and thought it was good."

I Can See Kitty: Written on the same page as the poem 'Retreat'. Written, it seems, for Jonathan Paton as a child.

Hal: Hal Burns.

LAST JOURNEY: RETURN

REFLECTIONS

Sonnet ("I saw Them playing . . ."): *Natal University College Magazine*, 10, 1924, p.26. In a version sent from Paton to Edward Callan the last line reads: "'This is mine,' He Said."

Sterility: Written on the same page as 'School' which is dated 1928.

Evening: *Natal University College Magazine*, 20, 1929, p.98.

Retreat: Found in an exercise book which contains an essay on 'The Afrikaner' which was probably written in 1941. The poem calls up another image of an Anglo-Boer War soldier's grave.

The Incurable: An earlier version exists of this poem in a handwriting which appears close to that of Paton in the early 1930s.

Death: *Natal University College Magazine*, 26, 1932, p.29.

Only the Child is No More: *Knocking on the Door*, 1975, p.64. Of this poem Paton says: "Nearly forty years later I wrote a poem for him [Paton as a child]. After thirteen years of living in the high interior I went to live at Anerley on the south coast of Natal. One afternoon I stood on the beach watching the swells come in. They rise and rise, taller and taller, and then become rollers, translucently green, and the white foam blows off the racing crests. Then they curl over, and after a moment of suspense they crash down, filling the air with their roaring." (*Towards the Mountain*, p.39)

The World is Changing too Fast for Me: Written on the same page as 'Anxiety Song of an Englishman' (above) which suggests that it was written around January 1949. The political context of the poem seems to recall the racial riots in Natal during this time (see 'I ask you, Indian people . . .').

1950-1984: This poem is based on an untitled and unfinished poem which Paton wrote in 1950 (see *Alternative Versions and Workings* above).

NOTES ON CONTRIBUTORS

PETER KOHLER

Peter Kohler was born in Zimbabwe in 1956, but lived in Lusaka and Johannesburg as well. He was educated, initially, at Thomas More High School in Kloof, Natal, and then at the University of Natal. After studying for a BA Honours (English), he received an MA degree from the University of Toronto. He is at present completing a PhD at the University of Cape Town, which focuses on the poetics of history and landscape in the work of Alan Paton. He is a lecturer in the English Department of the University of the Western Cape.

EDWARD CALLAN

Edward Callan was born in Ireland and educated there as well as in England, South Africa and the United States. Dr Callan is at present Distinguished University Professor, Emeritus, at Western Michigan University, Kalamazoo, where he received the Distinguished Faculty Scholar Award in 1980. He has been a member of St. Antony's College, Oxford University, and Visiting Professor of English at the University of Michigan. In 1983 he received the Distinguished Faculty Award from the Michigan Association of Governing Boards.

Dr Callan has written extensively on Alan Paton, whom he knew for many years. He compiled and edited Paton's political writings in *The Long View* (1967), and he provided the introduction to the 1987 Collier Books edition of *Cry, the Beloved Country*. His Twayne's World Authors Series volume, *Alan Paton* (1968), was listed by *Choice: Books for College Libraries* among the "Outstanding Academic Books of 1969"; it was updated in 1982.

Dr Callan's other works include *Auden* (Oxford University Press 1983), *Yeats on Yeats* (Dublin: Dolmen Press 1981) and a play on WB Yeats, *I Am of Ireland*. His writings on South Africa include the monograph, *Albert John Luthuli and the South African Race Conflict* (Western Michigan University Press 1962 and 1965).

DOUGLAS LIVINGSTONE

Douglas Livingstone was born in Kuala Lumpur, Malaya, in 1932. He qualified as a bacteriologist in Rhodesia in 1958, and since 1964 has lived in Durban, where he has worked on marine pollution, and has published several scientific papers. He is one of South Africa's most highly regarded contemporary poets. His work is known and published internationally and has won major awards both in the United Kingdom and in South Africa.

Works include: *A Littoral Zone* (1991); *The Anvil's Undertone* (1978); *A Rosary of Bone* (1975); *Eyes Closed Against the Sun* (1970); *Sjambok and other Poems* (1969); *Poems* (1968) (with Thomas Kinsella and Anne Sexton) and *The Skull in the Mud* (1960).

EDITOR'S AFTERWORD

AFTERWORD

VOICES

In a sense a book, like the world, is filled with voices, different kinds of voices. The one feature that seems to stand out above all others in Alan Paton's work is that of 'the voice', whether it is Msimangu's reading the Bible in *Cry, the Beloved Country* [*CBC*], or Paton's own, delivering a political lecture with its characteristic accent, timing and asides. It is, also, 'the voice' — and the language of the voice — that appears as the source of morality and action in his fiction. What we notice, for example, about the man who dupes Stephen Kumalo of his bus fare in Johannesburg, is his voice: he "spoke courteously, though in a strange Zulu." It is the peculiarity of his voice (his language is "strange") that reveals his dishonesty; or it is the discrepancy between his "strange" language and his voice ("spoke courteously") that makes the narrator suspicious of him. The voice, then, resonates throughout Paton's work in a way that suggests that it is the loadstone, pulling his narratives into line.

Songs of Africa, too, is commanded by the 'genre' of the voice. On closer inspection, though, it seems that 'the voice' is not so much singular, male and homogenous, as multiple, cross-gendered, even splintered. In place of the voice we need now to talk of voices. (We should, of course, put the words 'voice' and 'voices' in inverted commas because they are not really voices, but merely signs, traces, inscriptions of what we imagine to be the expressions of 'real' people.)

To the ear some of these voices here may seem light, barely audible, even unfamiliar, while others may sound deep, authoritative, almost imposing. At times they appear to have congregated around a singleness of purpose, a vision, but at other times they sound vague, confused, abstract. There are also voices here that speak in harmony — lyrical voices — while there are others that seem to know only the language of dissonance, difference. Most of the voices, though, speak through Paton, lying just behind the words that he speaks; sometimes they are barely audible at the margins of his voice, and at odd moments they upstage him, claiming his voice, his centre. However, it is always the voice of Paton that comes out on top, that asserts its influence over the poetic narrative.

There are also voices in this book who announce themselves in a language that is binary — the movement between opposing terms, the clash of opposites — while there are others who speak in a way that is indirect, playful, without polarity or hierarchy. There are voices, too, who, having captured the ears of the world, now mark time by repeating themselves — to speak differently would be to threaten the *status quo*. There are also eloquent voices whose words seem to float, while there are the inarticulate ones whose words fall like stones, and (to speak in a Patonesque cadence) in falling are sometimes broken. There are other voices who, once having spoken an indelible language, have found themselves in the court of history and those who, having been judged to have spoken wrongly, now appear desperate or resigned, waiting for some permanent

204

or comprehensive silence to cover them up — the voice of Verwoerd, parodied in 'Dr Verwoerd my boss my boss', is one of the easier examples to identify here. Sometimes there are voices who will speak or seek to speak of themselves in the form of an original identity, unified, nationalised; at other times there are voices whose language bears witness to identities which are slippery, multiple, heterogeneous, at times schizophrenic. There are voices, too, that consciously speak of themselves in the language of morality, politics, culture, history, while there are others who seem oblivious of metaphysics, and the language of metaphysics — Paton's voice in POEMS FOR CHILDREN, for example.

Some of the voices appear like spectres or ghosts between the covers of this book. They are long since dead and speak to us through fleeting images, memories, gestures, mute signals — the Anglican Archbishop Geoffrey Clayton, or the liberal philosopher Alfred Hoernlé, for example. Like all voices, all forms of inscription, they are always at the point of disappearing, constantly under erasure. However, it is at the point of erasure that they, paradoxically, make their invisible presences felt, which is why, in the first place, they appear as spectres, ghosts, disembodied forms. There are also those voices who are alive and well, and who sign themselves boldly, optimistically, as presences on the page — heedless of the future.

In short, it is possible to *decipher* a myriad voices in this book. Within each voice there is a struggle with words and identity. There is a desire to be born and a desire to discover whose 'voices' (or histories) they are. In all the voices that speak to us here, though, there is language, or particular languages. JM Coetzee writes about his discovery that "languages spoke people, or at least spoke through them", and that one might find oneself regarding even the language that one spoke with suspicion.

It is unlikely that Paton would have doubted the language that he spoke, but there is, in the way that the voices speak language in this book, a suggestion that for Paton language is dynamic, is active in the construction of meaning. (That language is not simply a mechanical mapping of words onto objects in the world.) There is also a sense of cultural relativity in Coetzee's rememberings. This is a feeling that any colonial son (like Paton) could have shared, living as a settler on the tip of Africa, trying to come to terms with its cultural and geographical differences and with the aggressiveness of colonial history. However, it is to this sense of both the centrality and fluidity of language that we can look, I would suggest, in order to begin to grasp Paton's own peculiar style, vocabulary, rhythm, syntax.

This book, then, like the world is filled with voices that are spoken through language. The most audible — because it is the focus of the other voices, and because it speaks with a particular kind of lyrical and institutionalised authority — is Paton's, of course. In a sense Paton's voice needs no introduction — it can speak for itself, and has been spoken for by others, including himself, on many occasions — and yet it is because of its authority, its public status, that it will insist, and rightly so, on being talked about once again. Although this buoyancy in Paton's voice is partly a result of its public profile, its authority, it is also connected with the way voices from the past are being re-articulated today —

some louder than others — as part of the post-apartheid story. That Paton had always envisaged a time when Apartheid would come to an end — the question was *when* not *if* — goes to support my claim that his place in the re-articulation of democratic voices is long overdue. And although Paton's voice has never disappeared from public view (*Cry, the Beloved Country* is still a popular seller), no voice is chiselled once and forever in stone: histories shift, signs change, cultures re-arrange and redefine themselves and in doing so change the inflections of the voices that they call up to speak for them or on their behalf. To read Paton today is to be alert to these shifts and changes in the public address.

LANGUAGE AND THE PATONESQUE

To introduce Paton's voices is to speak as a ventriloquist. It is difficult not to speak his language; it is difficult not to fall into the Patonesque intonation; as it is difficult to not allow his language to shape what one is trying to say. Sometimes, of course, one may resist the temptation, if not the pressure; sometimes not. The strengths and the potential dangers of finding Paton's language speaking us, can be seen in this passage from Peter Alexander's *Alan Paton: A Biography* — the most authoritative book on Paton's life and (along with Edward Callan's *Alan Paton*) on his work as well. It is a description of driving to meet Alan Paton 'in the flesh':

> I followed her [Anne Paton] meticulous instructions on the trip down in a rickety borrowed car, taking the highway from Johannesburg to Durban, turning off at Pietermaritzburg, following the signs to Hillcrest. I knew I was close when the road began winding up into the hills, rolling round hills green with thick grass in which the wide-horned red-and-white cattle wandered knee-deep, the valleys between the hills dark with native bush. When I stopped for a moment to look at a particularly striking view, the silence beat on my ear like a drum, except that below I could hear a stream tinkling over its black stones as it dropped into the Valley of a Thousand Hills. On the hillsides and surrounded by patches of bare earth, red as wounds, were the beehive huts of the Zulus, and occasionally a euphonious voice was upraised in a long, high-pitched cry designed, like a yodel, to carry from one mountain to another. This was Alan Paton's Natal, the area in which he had spent most of his life, and which he had transformed, in *Cry, the Beloved Country*, into one of the sacred places of the mind.
>
> (p.XVI)

This is an engaging narrative. Alexander is re-dramatising the aura of Paton and the Patonesque: through it we are able to relive what it must have been like to both meet Paton 'in the flesh', and to have read *CBC* for the first time in those heady days of liberal idealism. It is the genre of the biography which is the biographer's right to exploit. However, it also highlights what happens when this language — this Patonesque moment — is pushed to the extreme, pushed far enough for it to begin to draw attention to itself as a language, as a convention. In other words, it is a passage which pays its deepest respects to Paton, but it

206

also pushes the language far enough to make one conscious of the gap between what is being described and the words themselves. The gap is highlighted in the extent to which the language plays with perspective and proportion — at times straining to hit the right mark. In order to create the right effect boundaries are blurred, while depths and surfaces become unstable. We have, for example, a hyperreal image of "wide-horned red-and-white cattle" who wander knee-deep in the long grass (are they close to the road?), and with the emphasis on the diminutive we are told of "a stream tinkling over its black stones as it dropped" into the Valley of a Thousand Hills (is the word "dropped" not too strong here?). The point of perspective — regulated by Anne Paton's precise instructions — is high up but lost within itself, within the language, images, metaphors of the Patonesque (within the 'sacred place of the mind') as it attempts to capture in the right form and the right colour the landscape lying before it. What we have here is not so much a description of the landscape of the Valley of a Thousand Hills but Paton's landscape of the mind regulated by his language, and Alexander's replaying of that language. The phrase "patches of bare earth, red as wounds" is our signal to forage carefully around these words.

This, however, is not a criticism of Alexander's scholarly book, but it is rather a point about the way nature gets represented, how conventions are used, in a Paton-like language. It is a comment, in other words, on how this 'sacred place of the mind' constructs a picture for itself, and about what happens when the language doesn't quite cover the whole canvas. There are moments in CBC, too, that point to a similar difficulty that Paton appears to experience in making the Natal landscape fit into the language and the conventions that he adopts. For example, we have descriptions of rivers and mountains in both CBC and Towards the Mountain but Paton needs to make certain asides in order to contain the possibilities of discrepancies being read into his narrative. In CBC the final comment in the Author's Note is this: "The Umzimkulu is called the 'great river', but it is in fact a small river in a great valley." In Towards the Mountain we have similar attention drawn to perspective and size, but in this case the equivocation turns on the distinction between hills and mountains: "The hills to the north, though we would not call them mountains, are big ones, and the trains from Durban to Johannesburg have to climb them." The hills of Pietermaritzburg are "big ones" but we sense that the narrative would work better if they were not in between; if, in short, they were bigger, more like mountains. The convention that Paton's language speaks (partly borrowed from the picturesque) aspires to describe a landscape in which the high points need to be mountains, and they in turn should be exotic, if not sublime. The question is to what extent can this convention of scale adopt itself to rolling hills? In other words, what we have is a representation of nature (landscape) in which the convention needs to be stretched a little, in order to fit into it what the author feels compelled to say.

This sense of not having a convention at hand to work within — of not having the right words to speak with — is reinforced by comparing CBC with changes Paton made to the original manuscript. In what could be regarded as an index of Paton's symbolic world, there appear four pictures hanging on the study wall of the late Arthur Jarvis. One is of the crucifixion of Christ, another is a portrait of Abraham Lincoln, and then there is a picture of Vergelegen and its white gables; finally there is "a painting of leafless willows by a river in a wintry veld." (CBC p.125)

What all four pictures have in common is their concern with authority, with symbolic authority. They exude moral lessons about influence and timing, which confronts an anxiety about not being able to address the right audience in the right place at the right time, in the right language. Their authority comes from being able to speak to an audience beyond their immediate context, and to speak with influence in spite of being out of joint with their own histories. In this way they speak with authority but — and this is the irony (the moral lesson) — not to the people that they would most naturally address, or represent. Christ is crucified by the very people he came to save, Lincoln too is assassinated and his 'Gettysburg Speech' which is now famous was initially regarded as a failure by the people whose interests it aimed to serve; the gables of Vergelegen, too, need to struggle for a place in the aesthetics of the African landscape; and the landscape of the wintry veld is unpeopled, and by implication only to be enjoyed from the outside (by outsiders).

The willow by the river in a wintry veld, furthermore, is a fixing of one convention upon another, which leads to the image having — like the gables — a split register, or an ambivalent relationship to the indigenous context. In the original manuscript, however, Paton edits this picture: 'gum trees' are replaced by "willows", which underscores his attempt to find, and define, a South African aesthetic for himself. In terms of the governing aesthetic, the image of gum trees next to a river appears less pleasing, less appropriate, than the more conventional image of weeping willows. Paton initially attempts to use the image of gum trees — which in effect were imported and grown for use in the gold mines — to defuse the dominant convention, to move the image away from its direct European import. Moreover, he attempts to use the image of gum trees in order to make the landscape appear more South African — less European but also less indigenous. In short, the gum trees give Jarvis' study more local colour. However, being a South African means for Paton not being a colonial, nor an indigene. Rather it means engaging with and becoming part of the indigenous landscape and its people through the rites of passage of settlerhood: "I take this Africa this continent/Unto myself . . ./And am penitent." he says in the poem, 'I take this Africa'. Going through the initiations means being repentant, but also learning to love Africa with a new language — discarding colonial attachments — and this would also explain his attachment in the 1930s and 1940s to settler history and to 'boer' history in particular. To be a South African means to be settled in Africa as part of Africa, grafted onto Africa, to be spoken through by the language of Africa as an African (but not in an exclusive sense).

In terms of a local, South African aesthetic, the willows appear sickly and weak, even clichéd. That Paton should at the last minute bow to the governing convention by eventually replacing the image of the gum trees with that of the

208

willows, and yet maintain the South African landscape of the wintry veld in the foreground, tells us something about the kind of debate he undertook with himself on what language to use in order to describe the South African landscape and its people. (It also suggests a certain unease with part of settler history, mining and its migrant labour for example.)

The four pictures, then, point to the kind of symbolic experiments that Paton was preoccupied with prior to CBC. The various stages of the working out of this symbolic language, moreover, are to be found in his poetry. In fact, part of the significance of Paton's poetry is the extent to which it unravels the inner symbolic debate, the shifts, experiments and changes that Paton undergoes prior to, and after, 1946. What is significant about his response to his search for an appropriate symbolic language — and the metaphor of the journey is largely associated with this search — is both Paton's ear for discord and his rugged directness (the phrase that comes up again and again in CBC is the "truth" above all else). He seems aware that in stretching and playing with conventions some things are bound to go wrong; discrepancies and gaps arise which, for the Christian realist, can't be ignored.

In a sense, this unease with inherited European conventions of landscape representation fits into another common colonial complaint, and that is that the African landscape tends to disappoint the expectations of the imperial eye; that the African landscape needs to be worked on, the image touched up, if only slightly, in order to prevent the danger of its potential blandness or irregularity, or its roughness, from spoiling the total aesthetic effect. Paton, of course, set himself in the early 1930s against such imperial conventions and its criteria of what constitutes a beautiful landscape — this is what makes him different — but nevertheless we find that the language that he brings to bear on how to represent the South African landscape is caught between trying to find the right vocabulary for a start, and having, in the main, to draw on European examples (from Grayson, Alpa of the Plough, Masefield, Wordsworth), that nevertheless serve him well but are never enough. Up to 1946 he can only in effect draw on a handful of local writers but they again prove inadequate to the ambitious task that Paton sets himself, which is to represent the landscape of Natal under the umbrella of the great (unified) South African novel: Campbell (whose conventions are in the main poetic not narrative), Schreiner (who writes mainly of the Karoo, which proves useful but it is not Natal), and a few others.

He does, though, team up with a few Natal University College friends, and together they begin to develop a way of representing the Natal landscape. (Neville Nuttall's *Trout Streams of Natal* (1947), and R.O. Pearse's *Barrier of Spears* (1973) need, I would suggest, to be read alongside that of CBC.) In many ways, through the convention by which they represent nature — a convention that combines the picturesque and the sublime — they are all engaged in exploring the limits and possibilities of their world and their language. More importantly, in 1946, when Paton writes CBC , they are all focused on a similar mission to transform the South African landscape, including its social landscape, into something more meaningful, more manageable. While Paton travels around Europe and North America writing his book, Pearse is mapping the Drakensberg (the Cathedral Peak area), which includes, along with Paton's son David, trying to find out what the highest peak in the area is. Nuttall, at the time, is travelling around the northern parts of Natal, as a school inspector. In many ways, through their various travels and through the languages and conventions they had worked on together at university, they begin writing the same kind of 'book' — all three books prove to be popular. Although dealing with different subjects their books seem to overlap in many ways; the point of overlap is their representation of nature. (Pearse's book only comes out in 1973, but he had already written *Empty Highways* (1933) of his honeymoon travels to Kenya and back. I would even suggest that *CBC* owes some of its genesis to a 'reading' of *Barrier of Spears*, even though it appeared almost 30 years after Paton's novel!)

If Paton, Pearse and Nuttall are engaged in similar projects, writing similar books, Paton is nevertheless able to take a step, a political step, that Diepkloof Reformatory (and his penal tour around Europe and North America just after the Second World War) provided, which Pearse and Nuttall were never in a position to take. The Diepkloof experience enables him to represent the landscape as peopled, as occupied by African people whose sense of community, linked to that of the land, is undermined by the settler politics. For both Nuttall and Pearse the landscape is in a sense empty, and although there is a deep respect for indigenous life in both, it is a respect, a formal respect, that lacks a sense of belonging to a common symbolic community. This is not an argument about Paton being more authentic politically or more liberal, or less prejudiced — reading *CBC* would confirm a number of prejudices about African people (pastoral and simple) that the writings of Pearse and Nuttall would overlook. The difference between Paton and the other two, then, is not narrowly a political one. It is one of perspective which has to do with a shift, or a break away, from a particular convention of seeing (representing) the South African landscape and its people, that does not allow the roving eye to fix and stabilise the image, formally. The people of Ndotsheni and 'Shanty Town' in *CBC*, for example, are not simply formal types but have an edge and a complexity about them that singles Paton's work out from that of his peers.

If one takes a look at the way the convention of the picturesque manifests itself in Pearse, and compares it to Paton's use of it, we will see this difference clearly. If we are to compare Pearse's Drakensberg — most images would do — to the opening passage of *CBC*, we will notice that Paton draws on the convention of the picturesque, but in a way that suggests that the point of perspective has changed, or become unfixed. For Paton, the locus of the symbolic eye has shifted; the single, winding view which slips across the water and up into the mountains, finally settling in the mist, the God-head, is replaced by an eye that is, momentarily, displaced, bewildered, questioning, reflective — it looks from the valley up the misty mountains and then back down to the valley again. It is the colonial view displaced, become reflective, aware of being looked at as it does the looking. Paton is able to control this sense of displacement by taking a 'Long View', or by stepping out of the frame by taking up a position above this world. This perspective stabilises the unsettling shifts in perspective by turning omniscient, by looking down at the world through the eye of God — which confirms Douglas Livingstone's notion of Paton's perspective lying close to that of the Logos, the meaning of the world according to the word of God. The difference between Paton and Pearse and Nuttall is that he — lacking their modesty — is willing to play God, the maker of meaning. He is daring enough to try to change or tamper with the rules of traditional perspective, and by implication, to change the politics of social interaction. By doing so he alters an inherited belief system. That Paton should be willing to play (not be) God, should come as no surprise — CBC is filled with the language of prophecy, and Paton speaks to J.H. Hofmeyr regularly about the saints and sainthood and measures his own life, at one point, against that of the Saint Vianey. He also writes to Hofmeyr, while at Diepkloof, saying: "I feel myself more and more called upon by God . . . [and] that I am in some way being, 'prepared'." It is the role of missionary, prophet, saint, author, who is willing to speak of the future, to speak in the language of the future, who is thereby able to redefine an order of seeing, who is able to break away from the discursive strings that hold Nuttall and Pearse back, that makes him different.

More importantly, to play God is not only to speak in the imperative, to speak with confidence in a language of the future, but it is also to use language in a new way. It has often been commented upon that Paton took his language from his study of the Bible; that Stephen Kumalo, for example, speaks a language that is simple, direct, organic, pastoral, trustworthy. However, although the Bible is a key text in Paton's vocabulary we need to look at how a biblical language can ground itself so successfully (in CBC, for example) in the social and political terrain of Johannesburg. We need to register, if only briefly, that the politics of Paton's 'simple English' also comes from the kind of social welfare work that he had come across at the South African Institute of Race Relations [SAIRR], and more particularly through the biologist Eddie Roux's literacy work for night schools. The basis of Roux's work was his elaboration of Ogden's 'Basic English' into what he calls 'Easy English'. Roux had written a small and inconspicuous book called *The Cattle of Kumalo* (1943) in which he puts his 'Easy English' programme into action. Paton reviewed it, taking immediately to its simple language — which both Roux and Paton felt to be uniquely African. He seemed to take to it because it was both lyrical and earthy, poetic and functional. Roux's language was end-directed, but, unlike Ogden's, not without style. Paton's attention to the Bible (particularly the King James edition) was not enough in itself to enable him to develop a language that was able to resonate so successfully in the ears of people both in and outside the country, and that in many ways enabled him to short-circuit inherited political and educational positions.

METAPHOR OF THE JOURNEY

There was no ready made collection or even selection of Paton's poems (except possibly the few poems in an invaluable book, *Knocking on the door*) to which we could turn — which we could reproduce without being faced with scholarly and organizational problems, watching it print and circulate itself from our easy chairs so to speak. The poetry was, in the main, uncollected and much of

211

it was unpublished, which means our role in the collection was more than simply academic. One of the organising principles we used in the *Songs of Africa* was the metaphor of the journey. The book is structured around six journeys which attempt to represent various moments in Alan Paton's 'poetic life'. To refer to Paton's life as poetic, however, is to draw attention to the value attached to the vocation of the poet, and to the significance of representation (in particular metaphor) in his work. The idea of the journey is, of course, drawn from the compelling presence it has in his writings — the titles of his two autobiographies speak for themselves: *Towards the Mountain* and *Journey Continued*. Any reader of *CBC*, for example, is compelled to follow Stephen Kumalo's journey first by train to Johannesburg and at last up the mountain on the eve of his son's execution.

Paton's recurrent image of journeying towards the mountain could be one place to start discussing the theme. That he should find this image so overpowering, could mean that we should be looking for its genealogy in both the social and symbolic circles that he was moving in before the writing of *Cry, the Beloved Country*. Two figures stand out here as constants for this time. One is the moral and political presence of J.H. Hofmeyr (to whom *CBC* is in part dedicated), and the other is the Bible. However, while working on this project I was struck not only by the symbolic significance of the 'Mountain' in Paton's writing, but also by its sheer presence, density, materiality. At one point, I began to suspect that the 'Mountain' stood not only for the Godhead (that which we strive for but never conquer) but also for Liberalism, if not the Liberal Party. It also seemed to me that the connection Paton had with Liberalism could only pass through two sources: people with whom he worked at Diepkloof (people on the 'Board' such as Edith Rheinallt-Jones) and the SAIRR, but this influence only really took shape once he was in Johannesburg (from June 1935). It seemed that liberalism (with a small l) appeared to play with Paton's consciousness much earlier on — possibly in the late 20s, particularly in his opposition to the jingoistic policies of colonial Natal. In other words, this source of liberalism seemed to come through various influences early on in Paton's student life: as a Students' Christian Association [SCA] member at the Natal University College, for example. However, important as it was for Paton, the SCA was less political and more welfare oriented, and it didn't strike me as the kind of organisation to take on a monumental symbolic presence, as the 'Mountain' does, in Paton's imaginative life. The idea that the image of the mountain stood for the politics of liberalism, meant that I needed to look beyond the SCA, but nevertheless to something attached to it.

It seemed to have something to do with someone (or something) who was able to combine the idea of service with politics. Of course, it could only come in the shape of Jan Hofmeyr, whom Paton had described as a particularly robust opposition in rugby as well: "To oppose him . . . was a profound physical experience." (We should also note that Hofmeyr represented a liberalism with a small l, to which Paton took without difficulty, but Liberalism with the capital L is something he struggled against, as he mentions in the note to the poem,

212

'The Joke'). Hofmeyr is the figure through whom Paton discovers liberalism - - this may explain the significance Paton attached to his book *Hofmeyr*, which he regarded as his best. It is through Hofmeyr that liberalism begins to appear like the Godhead but at the same time as 'real,' practical, tangible. The difficulty I faced, though, was to make the symbolic shift from Hofmeyr to liberalism in the form of an argument about mountains. It was, of course, possible to make the point in a roundabout way, but not without opening oneself to the danger of ignoring the symbolic weight of the mountain itself. If Hofmeyr was the clue to the idea that the mountain stood for the principles of liberalism — principles that by definition are both ideal and absolute — then it was to Hofmeyr I needed to turn. I went carefully through Paton's book on Hofmeyr (*Hofmeyr*) which at over 500 pages is a 'mountain' in itself, but with little success.

Paton, of course, did not draw much and when he did it was private and more in the form of doodling; a private, deeply psychological language. Looking for some sign of the connection between Hofmeyr and the symbol of the mountain in Paton's diaries, however, threw up nothing, and his doodles proved useful for other parts of my argument, but not this one. I then managed to work carefully through some of the archival material that Paton kept while writing *Hofmeyr*. And then, between the pages of an old school exercise book, I found this:

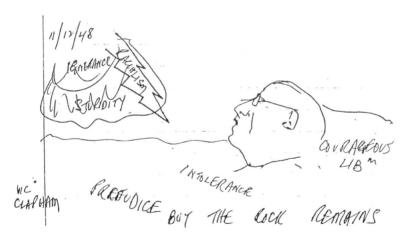

The writing reads — and we can decide in what order to read it: "Prejudice but the rock remains". Like the poem 'On the Death of J.H. Hofmeyr', it was drawn soon after Hofmeyr's death. Like the American Presidential heads (which include Lincoln) carved out of the stone at Mount Rushmore, Paton has carved his own particular memento here — a memento that enables "courageous liberalism" to stand against "racialism" ("ignorance", "stupidity") and "intolerance". The metaphor of the Mountain seemed to stand for liberalism in the shape of the head of Hofmeyr — its ideals and political realities. Hofmeyr represents courage and an institutionalised strength. It is no longer simply Isaiah's mountain of refuge and permanence but the mountain of liberal principles and fortitude. It is this image of liberalism that seems to provide much of the political and symbolic weight to CBC. However, once Liberalism, with a capital L, — as political party and doctrine — enters Paton's imagination he seems to struggle with his writing, with the workings of his imagination. The metaphorical playfulness of his language comes second to its more serious political message.

Peter Kohler
September 1995

INDEX OF FIRST LINES

A

A fine big fellow you are, my lad; 156
A knock there comes upon my door 158
After much exploratory 145
Ah! why do you come in the hours of dark 23
Allison Krause, for you this flower 99
Alone I sit upon the hollow throne, 143
And he said — it was two in the morning then — 77
Art lonely, son? see, the pale moon 14
As if unknowing of the sullen roar 53

B

Barefooted boy on Paumanok's shore 67
Black man standing weeping before me 82
Black man, we are going to shut you off 71
Black woman teacher in distant Bavendaland 85

C

Child, why did you come to me? 113
Confused no doubt by words like 'choose' 163
Could you not write otherwise, this woman said to 73
"Curlilocks, Curlilocks, will you be mine? 157

D

Dear Hal, I only want to say 167
Distant mumbling . . . 3
Doctors and nurses day by day 174
Down here where we talked of the Empire 81
Dr. Verwoerd my boss my boss 149

F

Far out the waves are calling, Marguerite 22
For the earth is corrupted, even the leaf and the 133
For unpermitted tramp of naked feet 10
From where the sun pours on the southern sand 54

G

Give me my sword — and gird it on, my son 38

H

He gazes on me with his long-dead eyes 2
Heavy with secret knowledge the earth turns 131
He's looking 106
Ho, Long One, what do you do? 140

I

I am myself an ordinary man 103
I am the Law, and the Power, and the Glory 89
I ask you, Indian people, where do you turn to now 81
I came to a valley where it was winter, and sat my 58
I can see Kitty 166
I do not claim to be like Brookes 150
I dreamt three students walked a road 11
I have approached a moment of sterility 65
I have barred the doors 141
I have seen my Lord in the forest, He walks from t 130
I have seen the ways of Death 175
I hear the noise of the loud laughing girls 74
I ran from the prison house but they captured me 33
I remember that you told me that you loved South A 79
I rise from my dream, and take suddenly this pen a 120
I saw the famous gust of wind in Eloff Street 127
I saw Them playing with Their bauble, Earth, 170
I see with passing of the tragic years 118
I sing the song of the Northward-bound 6
I take this Africa this continent 70
I'll stab the conscience of the world awake 87
I'm really quite good at remembering names 110
In the deep valley of the Umtwalumi 56
It has been said that Edgar's verse 164
It's quite clear that your manners 158

K

,Kyk ma, daar kom die ossewaens 48

L

Lady, won't you look at us 114
Let me relate a small affair. 144
Life was bitter, be that said 47

M

Makwela, Ikgopoleng, and you two Sibekos, 92
MESHAM! EDDINGTON! JEANS! Noble alliance! 158
Mkhumbane, awake, awake, the day is soon to break 100
Mkhumbane, it's time for sleep, it's time for eyes 116
Most Honourable I knock at your door 91
My apparently unwilling kookie 164
My friends are angry with me 142
My Lord has a great attraction for the humble and 128
My plan be in Thy mind, O God 136

216

N

Night is dark, leaving him unknowing 157
Night over farm, over furrow falling 45

O

O God my Maker, from whom all my gifts proceed, 137
O Lord give me thatgrace that I may so 135
Oh Lord, my enemies overwhelm me, they make me ash 134
Old walls that echoed to our cries 9
Olgan am I, first-born and noblest son of Til 39
On this great historic date 152
Once in the long dark hours of sleeping 24
Once in the Tavern of the Seas 144
Out of our father's land in former years 29

P

Peace on the meadowland, 171

R

Red dawn is in the desert 25
Retreat! Retreat! 173

S

Singer of childhood, do you remember 55
Sleep is the mocking thing when the mind's knot 34
Small boy I remember you 76
Small offender, small innocent child 36
Sometimes I was a glad lib 165

T

Tell me, What road are you going now? 97
The batteries are working and the great stamps roa 51
The bell it rings for you and me, 104
The black boy rose from his bed 86
The blood poured, bubbling like panthers 35
The Dutch may be a stolid race 163
The farmers know the peace of God 17
The grass-larks' call from the open veld 15
The lonely road winds on, and is lost in the mist 49
The man stood by the monument 87
The mist comes down from height and hill 57
The sea roars as ever it did 176
The slow marching 30
The sun goes trailing pitiless 16
The tributary widens, I sense an urgency in the wa 177
The village lies in Sabbath heat 32
The voice of God over Durban crying 78

The world is changing too fast for me. 177
The world is full of change and woe 112
There is a joy in dossing in a tent 5
There was a sweet family, Thorrold 155
There's memory of laughter, memory 157
There's no way carved yet, no applauding crowd 54
They leave the ploughshare and the sod 28
They say 'I must send you a present, my love, 95
. . . this old grey homestead by the road 50
This love is warm, knowing no artifice 35
This night a mother's son is called away 116
Thousands and thousands and thousands are marching 101
Toll iron bell toll extolling bell 96
Tugela, Tugela, sweep on, sweep on 52

U

Unto us a child is born 151
Upon the vlei the bull-frog croaks 46

W

We are the ones 108
We cogitate 162
We gave her a discardment 75
Welcome all, to 1982 153
We're the boys with the smart turn-out, 109
What is this sound from the world? These voices I 129
What, señor? — not want to go back? — if you knew! 41
When I was young my songs I sang 171
When the last sleep comes, lay me to rest 172
Where are your papers? Your papers? Your papers? 107
Where with his heavy-swinging trunk 27
Who likes me? 166
With man's first disobedience and the fall 26
With many very brilliant men 12

Y

You and I — 20
You, bus passenger, with the fat buttocks, 162
You, Indian woman in the rain, 77
You there, Luthuli, they thought your world was sm 98
Your prison in a word 44